OXFORD THEOLOGICAL MONOGRAPHS

D0068808

OXFORD THEOLOGICAL MONOGRAPHS

Probability
and Theistic Explanation

ROBERT PREVOST

CLARENDON PRESS · OXFORD
1990

Oxford University Press, Walton Street, Oxford OX2 6DP
Oxford New York Toronto
Delhi Bombay Calcutta Madras Karachi
Petaling Jaya Singapore Hong Kong Tokyo
Nairobi Dar es Salaam Cape Town
Melbourne Auckland
and associated companies in
Berlin Ibadan

Oxford is a trade mark of Oxford University Press

Published in the United States
by Oxford University Press, New York

British Library Cataloguing in Publication Data
Prevost, Robert W.
Probability and theistic explanation.
1. God. Existence
I. Title
212.1
ISBN 0–19–826735–5

Library of Congress Cataloging in Publication Data
Probability and theistic explanation / Robert Prevost.
(Oxford theological monographs)
Includes bibliographical references.
1. Theism.   2. Religion—Philosophy.   3. God.   I. Title.
II. Series.
BD555.P87   1990   211'.3—dc20   90–33121
ISBN 0–19–826735–5

Typeset by BP Integraphics Ltd, Bath, Avon
Printed in Great Britain by
Bookcraft (Bath) Ltd, Midsomer Norton, Somerset

ACKNOWLEDGEMENTS

I WANT to thank some of the many people who have helped me with this project: Prof. Basil Mitchell and Prof. Richard Swinburne for their careful supervision of my D.Phil. thesis, Mr Rom Harré and Mr J. R. Lucas for their patient tutorials through some very difficult material, Dr Charles Hughes for our many discussions on these topics, and Dr William J. Abraham for reading the penultimate draft and correcting many of its more obvious errors.

I would like to thank especially my parents, Dr and Mrs R. W. Prevost, Jr., whose support and encouragement made this essay possible.

CONTENTS

INTRODUCTION

It is recognized generally that traditional deductive arguments for the existence of God are fallacious or at best inconclusive. However, the recognition of this inadequacy does not constitute an admission that religious belief is thereby unjustified. A number of philosophers, while admitting of no compelling deductive argument for God's existence, consider religious belief to be justified on the basis of its power to explain some phenomenon or phenomena. Theism, on this account, is an explanatory theory, or hypothesis, whose acceptability is measured by its explanatory power.

Arguments to the best explanation have certain advantages which can be seen by contrasting them with more traditional arguments. Traditional deductive arguments involve at least one strong a priori causal principle as a premiss. Leibniz, for example, invokes the principle of sufficient reason in his cosmological argument: everything must have a sufficient reason for its existence. From this principle and an existential premiss, God's existence is inferred with logical certainty. Arguments with the deductive structure seek to demonstrate the existence of God in the strongest possible way.[1]

In contrast best-explanation arguments make a much weaker claim because they are based on an explanatory principle that is weaker than the principle of sufficient reason. J. J. Shepherd describes it this way: 'According to this principle one should press and go on pressing the question "why" until it becomes clear that to press it any further is plain silly.'[2] Best-explanation arguments are weaker than those based on the traditional a priori principles in a number of ways. First of all, they recognize that at the end of analysis there may be no explanation for a particular phenomenon. Eventually an impasse may be reached where it is no longer of any value to seek further explanations. It is not that the explanatory

---

[1] The most recent and best general discussion of deductive cosmological arguments in their various forms is William Lane Craig, *The Cosmological Argument from Plato to Leibniz* (London, 1980).   [2] *Experience, Inference and God* (London, 1975), 76.

2 INTRODUCTION

sequence is logically at an end, but rather that the point has been reached where the possible explanations on offer no longer answer our 'why' questions. With the traditional deductive arguments, Leibniz's for instance, the regress of reasons, or causes, cannot end until a sufficient reason, or final efficient cause, is found. The regress, given the truth of the a priori principle, must come to an end.

The explanatory arguments are weaker as well in a second way: they do not guarantee a unique answer to a 'why' question. Even in the case of questions about the existence and purpose of the universe, a variety of answers may be plausible at any given moment. Explanatory arguments allow for degrees of support for alternative explanations. An explanation may be a poor one or a good one; yet in both cases the explanation is supported by the evidence, even if only minimally. The theist, in claiming that the existence of God is the best explanation of the universe, admits that other explanations, or no explanation at all, are possible. But he believes that, among these alternatives, the existence of God most satisfactorily answers questions about the nature and existence of the universe pressed as far as possible. Deductive arguments, on the other hand, argue to an individual that is the uniquely logically possible sufficient reason for the existence of itself and the universe. Rational alternatives to theism, on this view, are not possible.

Often thinkers do not appreciate the shift from traditional deductive arguments to arguments to the best explanation. It is commonplace since Hume to counter deductive arguments by rejecting the a priori principles on which they are based. Thus, J. L. Mackie in evaluating Leibniz's cosmological argument comments: 'The principle of sufficient reason expresses a demand that things should be intelligible *through and through*. The simple reply to the argument which relies on it is that there is nothing that justifies this demand, and nothing that supports the belief that it is satisfiable even in principle.'[3] He concludes: 'The form of the cosmological argument which relies on the principle of sufficient reason therefore fails completely as a demonstrative proof.'[4] These comments are entirely appropriate

[3] *The Miracle of Theism* (Oxford, 1982), 85.   [4] Ibid. 87.

with regard to the deductive arguments, but they are inappropriate if applied to the explanatory arguments. Arguments to the best explanation do not assume that 'things should be intelligible through and through'. There may be no ultimate explanation. Nor do explanatory arguments assume that a unique answer to the quest for explanation exists, such as, with Leibniz, a being that was its own 'sufficient reason for existing'. Rather, explanatory arguments claim that of the possible alternatives there is a particular one which is best, even if other explanations are possible. Thus, the sort of objection Mackie makes to the deductive arguments does not apply to explanatory ones.

Some have attempted to apply the traditional objections to explanatory arguments. For example, Gary Doore criticizes an explanatory version of the teleological argument by asserting that it leads to an infinite regress of order-producing minds. He argues:

Then, by the same type of analogy as used, namely, an analogy based on the types of order produced by rational agents, we can conclude that it is probable (given that there is no better explanation) that the order of the postulated mind that produced the universe was itself produced by a rational agent, i.e., by another mind. But then there will be a series of mind-producing minds (since this second mind must have a cause—which by the analogical argument, will be a third mind—and so on), a series which must either go on to infinity or have an end in some first cause.[5]

Doore's comments reveal both the problem with his objection and the solution to it. He presumes that a principle as strong as the principle of sufficient reason is behind the regress of explanations. An infinite regress could occur only if of necessity there had to be an explanation for everything. However, nothing in the explanatory principle, as described above, warrants such a strong claim. The regress of explanations will go on only so far as there are better explanations (see his parenthetical remarks). If there is no better explanation, then there will be no danger of a vicious infinite regress. And that is just the claim of the theistic explanation: no further explanatory value is gained by going beyond God, and therefore there is no

---

[5] 'Further Reasons for Agreeing with Hume', *Religious Studies*, 16 (1980), 153–4.

point in trying. We can agree with Doore's comments about the explanatory regress, but not with his objection to this version of the teleological argument. His criticism is misplaced. What finds its force readily in the context of deductive arguments fails when applied to explanatory arguments.

Theism defended as the best explanation for a set of phenomena does not, then, have the same liabilities as when it is defended as the conclusion of a deductive argument (though it may have others). For this reason it is possible to reject traditional deductive justifications for religious belief while remaining confident that religious belief can be justified.

The best-explanation approach, however, is not without its problems. One very significant disadvantage is a certain confusion in the very idea of theism as an explanatory hypothesis. Arguments to the best explanation vary greatly, and this variety produces confusion about the nature of theistic explanation. This is brought on in part because the concept of explanation is used imprecisely. 'Explanation' sometimes refers solely to the causal antecedents and conditions for the existence of some particular state of affairs. In most instances of scientific explanation, this is the sense of explanation used. We explain a phenomenon's occurrence by reference to these antecedents. For example, we explain tidal phenomena by reference to the gravitational forces of the moon.

This use of the concept as specifically causal explanation needs to be distinguished from a use of the concept more broadly conceived as making a state of affairs intelligible. The difference between the two uses lies in the fact that, though all causal explanations make a state of affairs intelligible, not all explanations that make things intelligible are causal explanations. Sometimes we seek to explain causally a state of affairs. We may explain a shattered window by drawing attention to the ball that was thrown through it. But though at times we seek to make something intelligible by an appeal to a cause, as in the case of the shattered window, at other times we seek sorts of explanation which, though not causal, serve to clarify and to enlighten. For example, we may explain why a particular historical document such as the Magna Carta is so significant, or we may explain how a word is used properly in the language. These explanations make intelligible a state of affairs, but not by invoking causes.[6]

The distinction between these two sorts of explanation marks, however roughly, the contrast between two particular versions of theistic explanation which can be found in the literature. The first is modelled on causal explanation. God, it is claimed, causally explains the existence of some phenomenon such as the universe. R. G. Swinburne is the clearest proponent of theistic explanation conceived of this way. He defines explanation in terms of causation: 'What is it to provide a true explanation of the occurrence of a phenomenon E? It is to state truly what (object or event) brought E about (or caused E), and why that was efficacious.'[7] In turn he defines theistic explanation causally: 'all important *a posteriori* arguments for the existence of God have a common characteristic. They all purport to be arguments to an explanation of the phenomena described in the premises in terms of the action of an agent who intentionally brought about those phenomena.'[8]

A second version of theistic explanation, which will be designated as integrative explanation, takes explanation as 'making intelligible'. Religious belief, on this view, is a coherent system of propositions which make intelligible the universe. This is the kind of explanation that, for example, Keith Ward seems to espouse. On the arguments for the existence of God he comments: 'These are not proofs, in the sense of arguments which no one can deny. They are attempts to show how the idea of God, as a self-existent being with a rational moral purpose, can make sense of various puzzling features of our world.'[9] Basil Mitchell also appears to have this sort of explanation in mind when he asserts that 'the theist is urging that traditional Christian theism *makes better sense of* all the evidence available than does any alternative on offer'.[10] Ian Ramsey more clearly supports this view. He understands the purpose of metaphysical inquiry as the elaboration of 'some explicit interpretative scheme critically suited as far as may be

---

[6] I discuss the nature of integrative explanation in greater detail in ch. 6.
[7] *The Existence of God* (Oxford, 1979), 22.
[8] Ibid. 19–20.   [9] *Holding Fast to God* (London, 1982), 27.
[10] *The Justification of Religious Belief* (London, 1973), 40 (my italics).

to the whole of experience.'[11] On this view, religious belief, and *a fortiori* theistic belief, is an interpretative theory which provides the categories by which the universe is understood.

Many discussions fail to distinguish clearly between these two sorts of theistic explanation. Consequently, many thinkers ignore the explanatory power of theism as an integrative explanation and evaluate the explanatory power of theism in the narrow sense of causal explanation only. Two examples will illustrate this point. Recently Alvin Plantinga has tried to refute certain assumptions about the relationship between evidence and religious belief.[12] The evidentialist objection to theistic belief, as he describes it, claims that, in order to be rational, belief in the existence of God must be based on proper evidence; but it is not so based; therefore, belief in God is irrational. One obvious way of countering this objection is to argue that in fact theistic belief is based on proper evidence. But Plantinga queries the idea that a belief, to be rational, must be based on evidence at all. It is in the context of arguing against certain views of evidence and belief that he broaches the notion of theistic explanation. He accepts that some hold theistic belief to be a hypothesis 'designed to *explain*' something. Belief in God would be acceptable on that account, if it were adequately supported as the best explanation of the phenomenon. Plantinga attacks this view as untenable. He writes:

Now from this point of view, most of the beliefs characteristically accepted by, say, Christians are peculiarly ill-founded. How could the existence of a triune God, or the incarnation of the Second Person of the Trinity, or the death and resurrection of the Son of God be sensibly thought of as *hypotheses* designed to explain what we find in *B* [i.e. the universe]? What, in *B* do these things explain? Could one sensibly claim they are worthy of belief because of their high probability with respect to *B*, or because they explain some significant portion of *B*? Obviously not.[13]

---

[11] 'On the Possibility and Purpose of a Metaphysical Theology', in Ian Ramsey (ed.), *Prospect for Metaphysics* (London, 1961), 154.

[12] See his 'Reason and Belief in God', in Alvin Plantinga and Nicholas Wolterstorff (eds.), *Faith and Rationality* (Notre Dame, Ind., 1983), 16–93, and his 'The Probabilistic Argument from Evil', *Philosophical Studies*, 35 (1979), 1–53.

[13] 'The Probabilistic Argument', p. 51.

Plantinga contends that religious beliefs such as the trini-
tarian concept of God cannot be construed in any sense as
explanations. What, he asks, could they explain?

Plantinga's criticism is a forceful one, but it has merit only
against a particular view of theistic explanation, the view based
on causal explanation. Perhaps, as he claims, certain specifically Christian doctrines are not and could not be hypotheses
postulated to explain causally some evident natural phenomenon in experience. But if theistic explanation is considered as
an integrative explanation, this objection seems less forceful.
Christian theism, when taken as a systematic interpretative
theory, provides the categories by which experience is understood. In so far as a particular dogma such as the redemptive
incarnation is essential to Christian theism, it has explanatory
value if the entire Christian belief system has value in making
sense of the universe.

Mackie makes a similar mistake in his evaluation of theism.
He notes that arguments can be both deductive and non-
deductive, and that both kinds of argument are utilized in
support of or in rejection of belief in God. Furthermore, he
describes non-deductive arguments as arguments to the best
explanation:

But most of the arguments on either side . . . include important non-
deductive elements. Each of them starts from various pieces of evidence or considerations about some part of our experience, and in
many cases the conclusions clearly go beyond what is contained, even
implicitly, in the premises. All such arguments can be seen as resting
on one general principle, or as sharing one basic form and purpose:
they are arguments to the best explanation. The evidence supports
the conclusion, it is suggested, because if we postulate that that conclusion is true—or better, perhaps, that it is at least an approximation
to the truth—we get a more adequate overall explanation of that
whole body of evidence, in the light of what ever considerations are
cited, than would be given by any available alternative hypothesis.[14]

Mackie's description of arguments to the best explanation is
a general one, applicable to all kinds of explanation. However,
like Plantinga, he does not distinguish causal explanation from
other sorts of explanation. When he assesses the value of theistic explanation with respect to the variety of evidence, he

[14] *The Miracle of Theism*, p. 4.

assumes that the acceptability of theism will be a function of its power to explain the evidence causally.[15]

Mackie makes no reference at all to theism as an integrative hypothesis. He simply ignores the value of theism for making sense of the data of the universe.

Plantinga and Mackie are not alone in their error. There is in general a lack of critical discussion of theism as an integrative explanation. And reasons for this are not hard to find. In the first place, the very idea of integrative explanation is ambiguous. Mitchell, for example, states that theism makes better sense of the data of the universe and gives numerous examples to illustrate his meaning. But, even though everything at issue depends on an interpretation of 'makes better sense of', he makes no explicit attempt to interpret the phrase. Though Ramsey's discussion of metaphysics as a 'map' of the universe is somewhat less vague, he does not discuss specifically how this 'map' explains.

What complicates the issue is that different metaphors are utilized to communicate the basic idea behind integration. Each of the concepts of 'world-view', 'paradigm', 'language game', and 'metaphysical map' expresses, among other things, the idea of integration.[16] Not everyone who uses these concepts sees religious belief as an explanatory hypothesis. But many do, and in both cases, fideist and non-fideist alike, the use of these concepts reflects a concern to characterize religious belief as a systematic approach to life and experience. The richness of the imagery, however, does not facilitate understanding. The very existence of such diversity presents a barrier to anyone attempting to understand and evaluate religious belief so construed.

A second reason for the lack of discussion of theism as an integrative explanation is the apparent difficulty in evaluating explanations, or systems, of this type. We have but to observe the sheer abundance of literature on the epistemic status of

[15] *The Miracle of Theism*, pp. 251–2.
[16] For various alternative ways to apply Wittgensteinian ideas to religious belief, see W. D. Hudson, *The Philosophical Approach to Religion* (London, 1974), Patrick Sherry, *Religion, Truth, and Language Games* (London, 1977), and D. Z. Phillips, *The Concept of Prayer* (London, 1965). Ian Barbour uses the idea of a paradigm, popularized by Thomas Kuhn, in his examination of religious belief. See his *Myths, Models and Paradigms* (London, 1974).

language games and of paradigms to recognize the difficulties surrounding the issue of their justification. And though philosophers of religion have been quick to use these metaphors to describe religious belief, there has been little detailed philosophical discussion from a non-fideist position on how to evaluate religious belief construed as a metaphysical map, language game, or paradigm. Mitchell's contribution represents the noted exception to this state of affairs. In *The Justification of Religious Belief* he addresses explicitly the question of whether religious belief, taken as a conceptual system, can be supported rationally. However, in the relevant part of the book, he limits his discussion to the very specific issue of illustrating how arguments in support of theism proceed and showing that the procedure is a rational one. Except for a brief summary, he does not address the question of how religious belief in particular explains a phenomenon. As a consequence his conclusions leave many questions unanswered. In any case with the exception of Mitchell there is very little literature in the context of philosophy of religion concerned specifically with the problems associated with evaluating integrative explanations. This fact undoubtedly contributes to the general neglect of such explanations by the philosophical community.

A third reason for this neglect has to do, not with integrative explanation *per se*, but rather with the most recent arguments for or against theism. These have been uniformly arguments based on causal explanation. Shepherd, for example, argues that the continuing existence of the universe can be explained best by the constant choice by God to sustain the universe in existence. Hugo Meynell believes that the intelligibility of the universe is explained best by the fiat of 'something analogous to human intelligence in the constitution of the world'.[17] And the most important recent contributor, Swinburne, defines theistic explanation, as we noted above, 'in terms of the action of an agent who intentionally brought about those phenomena'. Each of these individuals takes the fundamental explanatory relation to be causality, and each sees the action of God as causally explaining, in the case of Meynell and Shepherd, some particular phenomenon or, as with Swinburne, some group of

---

[17] Cf. Shepherd, *Experience, Inference and God*, ch. 4, and Hugo Meynell, *The Intelligible Universe: A Cosmological Argument* (London, 1982), 68.

phenomena. This recent emphasis on causal explanation has directed the attention of commentators toward theism as a causal explanation and away from theism as an integrative explanation. Thus, as the example of Mackie illustrates, few attempt to assess the theistic hypothesis conceived of in this latter way.

For these and other reasons one can understand the current state of affairs. This situation is, nevertheless, unfortunate. Causal explanation, though a very important sense of the concept of explanation, does not represent entirely the sense intended in many references to theism as an explanatory hypothesis. Any argument for the existence of God is bound to fail to capture the full explanatory power of theism if that argument is based solely on the strength of theism as a causal explanation. This, I believe, is the central difficulty of Swinburne's recent contribution. Though his discussion is of exemplary clarity and rigour, his conclusion lacks persuasiveness. This lack is due in part to his methodology, but also in part to his use of causal explanation as the sole model for theistic explanation.

My intention in this essay is to address these fundamental issues, which have led to the neglect of theism as an integrative explanatory hypothesis. To begin this I shall examine the recent work of Swinburne. He goes to great lengths to spell out the content of the theistic hypothesis, the sort of explanation it is, and the criteria and methodology necessary to evaluate the evidential support for theism. His argument in each instance is lucid and forceful; and as a consequence he has presented one of the most powerful arguments for the existence of God given in recent years. I shall take his argument as the principal example of the sort of causal explanation to which I object.

Over against Swinburne I shall argue two basic themes. I shall maintain, first, in contrast to his Bayesian analysis, that there exists a logic of informal reasoning which, when uncovered, is sufficient to guide rational discrimination between integrative explanations. I shall maintain, secondly, that theism construed as an integrative explanation has greater potential explanatory power than theism construed as a strictly causal explanation.

The two accounts of theistic explanation do not differ at

every point of substance necessarily. For example, they may share similar concepts of God. By both accounts, God is the ultimate source of existence, the creator and sustainer of all things other than himself, and therefore the cause of all things. And certain problems as well are common to both versions. The presence of evil will be problematic for both accounts of theism. Nevertheless, in spite of their common ground, the alternatives diverge significantly, and this divergence is most evident with respect to issues concerning the nature and evaluation of explanation. Since the strength of the hypothesis is a function of the power of the hypothesis to explain, different views of explanation will imply different ideas of how that power should be evaluated. Hence, the particular points at issue between the two views revolve around the nature of theistic explanation: what sort of explanation it is, what is the content of the theistic explanation, and how such explanations are evaluated. To the extent that Swinburne defines the theistic explanatory hypothesis in the more narrow causal sense, the thrust of my criticism will be that he cannot exploit the full explanatory power of theism.

I

EVIL AND THEISTIC EXPLANATION

I HAVE noted the existing confusion over the nature of theistic explanation. This confusion results in part from the problem presented by the justification of religious belief. Often it appears to be taken for granted that religious beliefs, for example, that God exists or that salvation is mediated exclusively through Jesus, are incapable of justification. Beliefs of this type, it is claimed, cannot be proved. They are matters for faith, not reason, and, therefore, are objects of commitment, not rational assessment.[1]

This opinion is strengthened if religious belief is taken to be a world-view, language game, or paradigm. Standards of evaluation, it is believed, are internal to the world-view, language game, or paradigm. There are no external standards with which religious beliefs can be assessed. Therefore, religious beliefs are fundamental and basic; and, though they can form the basis for criticism within a world-view, they themselves cannot be justified.[2]

Swinburne challenges this received wisdom about the justification of religious belief. Since theism is an explanation for various phenomena, he claims, we can use the same tools for evaluating the theistic hypothesis as those utilized by scientists for evaluating large-scale scientific theories. In particular Swinburne uses the criterion of simplicity and Bayesian confirmation theory (henceforth called the Bayesian methodology) for determining the relevant probabilities of competing explanations.

This methodology is exceptionally clear and rigorous, and it is evident that his argument for the existence of God presents a serious hurdle for non-theists. But there are reasons to doubt whether these tools are appropriate for assessing some kinds of

[1] Cf. W. W. Bartley, III, *The Retreat to Commitment*, 2nd edn. (London, 1984), 3–8.
[2] Cf. Phillips, *The Concept of Prayer*, and John Hick, *Faith and Knowledge*, 2nd edn. (New York, 1966), 151–211.

evidence and some kinds of theistic explanation. If this doubt is justified, then there is reason to suspect that he has not provided as strong an argument for the existence of God as is possible. Furthermore, the failure of the Bayesian assessment of the theistic hypothesis will lead to a more adequate characterization of the sort of explanation theism is.

The issue I want to address in these first two chapters is the use of Bayes's theorem as a general methodological tool for evaluating the evidence for theism. In this chapter I argue that the use of the theorem leaves the evaluation of theism's explanatory power incomplete. An analysis of the problem of evil reveals that assessing the explanatory power of theism does not always follow the Bayesian pattern: explaining why God allows evil requires some non-Bayesian method for evaluating explanatory power. Hence, a straightforward application of Bayes's theorem does not accurately represent the evidential significance of evil.

I

Evidence makes a hypothesis to some degree probable, or likely to be true. The degree of this probability can vary from evidence to evidence and from hypothesis to hypothesis. So in any particular case a specific piece of evidence may make one hypothesis more probable than it makes another hypothesis. And in another case, with another piece of evidence, this order may be reversed. The second piece of evidence may make the second hypothesis more probable than it makes the first. However, though these evidential-support relationships can vary greatly, they are not indeterminate. Rules exist which describe how much probability a hypothesis has on given evidence. Confirmation theory is the study of these rules. As Swinburne describes it, 'Confirmation Theory seeks to state the rules for different evidence conferring probability on different hypotheses.'[3]

One of these rules which Swinburne uses to assess theism is Bayes's theorem. This theorem, which follows from the axioms of the probability calculus, makes explicit which factors are important for the evaluation of a hypothesis. Stated briefly,

[3] *An Introduction to Confirmation Theory* (London, 1973), 1.

according to Bayes's theorem, the probability of the hypothesis given the evidence is equal to the prior probability of the hypothesis multiplied by the value of its explanatory power.[4]

This statement of the theorem includes two technical concepts: prior probability and explanatory power. In order to help clarify these concepts, we might consider a simple hypothesis: 'Fido, my dog, chewed my shoes' is a hypothesis postulated to explain the current state of the shoes. The prior probability of this hypothesis is the probability of the hypothesis before the specific evidence is considered. The question is, how likely is it, generally speaking, that Fido would have chewed my shoes. A number of different considerations come to bear in calculating this probability. To use one example, Fido may have a history of chewing shoes, and, therefore, we would expect beforehand that he would do it again. Given Fido's history, then, the prior probability of the hypothesis would be high.

We want also to know how powerful an explanation the Fido hypothesis is. Explanatory power is the value of the ratio between the probability of the predictive power of the hypothesis and the prior probability of the evidence. The predictive power of the hypothesis is the probability of the existence of the evidence given the truth of the hypothesis. The 'Fido' hypothesis has great predictive power since it entails the fact that the shoes were mangled. But explanatory power is also relative to the prior probability of the evidence. The prior probability of the evidence is the probability that the evidence would exist before considering the truth of the hypothesis. The relevant question with regard to the Fido hypothesis is whether there was any probability that the shoes would have been mangled in any way other than by Fido chewing them. If there is a high probability that some other process was operative which would have been likely to mangle the shoes, then the prior probability of the evidence would be high. If, for example, I jogged regularly over rough terrain, there would be a great chance that the shoes would be damaged anyway. But, if there

---

[4] If h is the hypothesis, e is the evidence, k is background knowledge (what is known apart from e), and $P(h/e . k)$ is the probability function stating the probability of the hypothesis given the evidence and background knowledge, then Bayes's theorem is as follows: $P(h/e . k) = P(h/k) . [P(e/h . k) / P(e/k)]$.

are no other reasons to expect the shoes to be in their damaged state other than the fact that Fido chewed them, the prior probability of the evidence is comparatively low.

With this example, we can see how, on the one hand, if the truth of the hypothesis entails or makes probable the occurrence of the evidence, the hypothesis has high predictive power; on the other, if the occurrence of the evidence is very unlikely except for the truth of the hypothesis, the prior probability of the evidence is low. The value of the explanatory power is a function of the ratio between the two: the greater the predictive power of the hypothesis, the greater the explanatory power; while the lower the prior probability of the evidence, the greater the explanatory power. The hypothesis that Fido damaged the shoes will have high explanatory power if its predictive power is high, that is, if the truth of the hypothesis would entail or make highly probable the existence of the chewed shoes, and if the prior probability of their existence is low, that is, if there were no other reason to expect the shoes to be damaged.

Bayes's theorem is an elegant way to assess the probability of a hypothesis given a specific set of evidence. If a numerical, or even simply a comparative, value can be assigned for the prior probability of the hypothesis and for those probabilities which determine the explanatory power of the hypothesis, then a value, similarly either numerical or comparative, can be assigned to the probability of the hypothesis on the given evidence.[5] Assessing a specific hypothesis on the evidence requires determining the particular values for the relevant probabilities. In the case of theism this will involve determining values for the prior probability of the theistic hypothesis, for the predictive power of theism relative to specific pieces of evidence, and for the prior probability of each specific piece of evidence.

The values of the particular probabilities are determined by different kinds of consideration. The value of the prior probability of the hypothesis is ascertained by applying specific evaluative criteria. For example, other things being equal, the more simple a hypothesis is, the more likely it is to be true.[6]

---

[5] Swinburne, *Confirmation Theory*, pp. 38–40; cf. Swinburne, *The Existence of God*, pp. 65–6.   [6] See ch. 2.

The same sort of reasoning applies to assessing the prior probability of the evidence. The more simple the evidence is, the more likely it is either to exist uncaused (in the case of the universe) or to be caused by a great number of things. Simplicity is especially important because, as Swinburne notes, it is the major factor in evaluating the prior probability of large-scale theories. But, for hypotheses of more narrow scope, the fit of the hypothesis with other knowledge and the scope of the hypothesis have some bearing on prior probability as well.

A different sort of consideration is involved in the evaluation of the predictive power of a hypothesis relative to a specific piece of evidence. The predictive power of a hypothesis is a measure of how likely it is that the evidence would exist if the hypothesis were true. According to Swinburne, if the hypothesis fully explains the evidence, the predictive power can be assessed on the basis of the completeness of the explanation. He defines full explanation in terms of deductive entailment: 'Now if there is a full cause C of E and a reason R which guarantees C's efficacy, there will be what I shall call a *full explanation* of E. For given R and C, there will be nothing remaining unexplained about the occurrence of E. In this case the "what" and the "why" together will deductively entail the occurrence of E.'[7] Since the evidence will follow by deductive entailment from the description of the hypothesis in a full explanation, the probability of the predictive power of the hypothesis is 1.

On this view, an assessment of the predictive power of a full explanation is relatively easy. More difficult is an evaluation of the predictive power of a partial explanation. In a partial explanation the factors cited in the hypothesis only facilitate or make probable the occurrence of the evidence.[8] The hypothesis alone will not deductively entail the evidence. For that reason the likelihood of the evidence given the hypothesis will be less than 1; and so, in a partial explanation other considerations

---

[7] *The Existence of God*, p. 24. Deduction is an end-point of probability. If e^1 entails e^2, then $P(e^2/e^1) = 1$. Cf. Swinburne, *Confirmation Theory*, pp. 35 f. on axiom I. Therefore, if h is a full explanation of e, then $P(e/h . k) = 1$.

[8] *The Existence of God*, p. 24. If h is a partial explanation of e, then $P(e/h . k) < 1$.

must come into play in order to assess how likely it is that the evidence would exist if the hypothesis were true.

This last point is important for Swinburne's argument because he does not propose to defend theism as a full explanation of the evidence. The hypothesis he defends is a minimal one. He describes it this way:

Note that I take *h* simply as 'there is a God'. *h* is not supposed for any of the *e* to provide a full explanation of *e*. . . . the existence of God does not fully explain, for example, the existence of the universe, which is the phenomenon cited by the cosmological argument as evidence of his existence. . . . We could of course have taken *h* as 'there is a God who had the intention of bringing about a universe', and then *h* would provide a full explanation of the existence of the universe and $P(e/h)$ [i.e. the predictive power of the hypothesis] would equal 1.[9]

This concession on Swinburne's part is significant. Because the theistic hypothesis is a partial explanation, there will be no straightforward deductive entailment between the theistic hypothesis and the evidence. Therefore, he must appeal to more complex considerations in order to assess the predictive power of the theistic hypothesis.

By applying the evaluative criteria and Bayes's theorem, Swinburne can assess with greater rigour the evidence for the existence of God. In the cosmological argument, for example, the existence of God is postulated to explain the existence of the complex physical universe. The existence of the universe, he argues, is something that science cannot explain. The universe, with its particular amount of matter governed by particular natural laws, by definition includes whatever natural laws that are involved in scientific explanation. Thus, the universe is far 'too big' for scientific explanation. It follows that two options are open with regard to the explanation of the universe: either the universe is completely inexplicable, that is, the universe simply is the brute fact of existence, or we must go beyond the universe to posit a non-scientific explanation for the existence of the universe.[10] In the assessment of the cosmological argument Swinburne is concerned to determine which of these options is supported best by the evidence of the existence of the complex physical universe.

According to Bayes's theorem, a hypothesis is confirmed by

9 Ibid. 69.   10 Ibid. 121–7.

the evidence if and only if the predictive power of the hypothesis with respect to the evidence is greater than the prior probability of the evidence.[11] Intuitively, this means that if evidence is to raise the overall probability of a hypothesis, the explanatory power of the hypothesis must be sufficient to raise the prior probability of the hypothesis. An increase in the probability of the hypothesis occurs if and only if the value of the explanatory power of the hypothesis is greater than 1. For this to be the case, the predictive power of the hypothesis must be greater than the prior probability of the evidence.

For an example we might consider evidence gathered for a court trial of a person suspected on a burglary charge. Suppose that, among other things, the police investigation found the suspect's fingerprints on a window in the room in which the crime was committed. The hypothesis is that the suspect left the fingerprints on the window at the time he committed the crime. The explanatory power of the hypothesis will be determined by how likely it is that the fingerprints would have been there if in fact the suspect had committed the crime, i.e. by the predictive power of the hypothesis, as compared to how likely the fingerprints would have been there anyway, i.e. the prior probability of the evidence. The extent to which the evidence confirms the hypothesis will be determined by comparing these relative values. If, for example, the suspect was a window-cleaner by trade and happened to be cleaning the windows of the room of the scene of the crime on the day of the crime, then the likelihood of his fingerprints being on the window would be high. This fact would indicate a high prior probability of the evidence and, consequently, would tend to lower the explanatory power of the hypothesis. On the other hand, if it were the case that ordinarily the suspect would not be at the scene of the crime, then it would be less likely that his fingerprints would be on the window except for the fact that he committed the crime. This fact would lower the prior probability of the evidence and would tend to raise the explanatory power of the hypothesis. In this manner, then, we see how the value of the explanatory power of a hypothesis is a function of its predictive power and the prior probability of the evidence.

[11] $P(h/e \cdot k) > P(h/k)$ iff $P(e/h \cdot k) > P(e/k)$. Cf. Swinburne, *Confirmation Theory*, pp. 48–9, principle c.

These implications of Bayes's theorem show that a hypothesis can be confirmed by the evidence on one or both of two considerations. Either the predictive power of the hypothesis can be high or the prior probability of evidence can be low. Considering the theistic hypothesis then, the existence of God will be confirmed by a specific piece of evidence if either that piece of evidence is such that it is expected in a universe created by God, that is, the hypothesis of theism has high predictive power with regard to the evidence, or that piece of evidence is not to be expected but for the action of God, that is, the prior probability of the evidence is low.

We see these considerations applied in Swinburne's assessment of the cosmological argument. The cosmological argument starts with the complex physical universe as evidence. Swinburne believes the existence of the universe confirms the existence of God because the existence of the universe has low prior probability. To argue this point he appeals to the criterion of simplicity. Simple things are more to be expected a priori than complex things. The universe, with its particular amount of matter arranged in various and diverse ways, is a very complex thing. He comments:

A complex physical universe (existing over endless time or beginning to exist at some finite time) is indeed a rather complex thing. We need but to look at our universe and meditate about it, and the complexity should be apparent. There are lots and lots of separate chunks of it. The chunks each have a different and not very natural volume, shape, mass, etc.—consider the vast diversity of the galaxies, stars, and planets, and pebbles on the seashore. Matter is inert and has no power which it can choose to exert; it does what it has to do. There is just a certain finite amount, or at any rate finite density of it, manifested in the particular bits; and a certain finite amount, or at any rate finite density of energy, momentum, spin, etc. There is a complexity, particularity, and finitude about the universe which cries out for explanation, which God does not have.[12]

Because the universe is so complex, its prior probability is very low. Though, as Swinburne admits, the predictive power of theism is not all that high relative to the existence of a complex physical universe, the prior probability of the universe existing uncaused is so low that the universe is unlikely to

[12] *The Existence of God*, p. 130.

exist other than by the action of God. For that reason the existence of the universe confirms God's existence. Swinburne summarizes the argument in this way:

It is very unlikely that a universe would exist uncaused, but rather more likely that God would exist uncaused. The existence of the universe is strange and puzzling. It can be made comprehensible if we suppose that it is brought about by God. This supposition postulates a simpler beginning for explanation than does the supposition of the existence of an uncaused universe, and that is grounds for believing the former supposition to be true.[13]

Therefore, we see how, by using these tools, namely, specific evaluative criteria and Bayes's theorem, Swinburne introduces a great amount of rigour to the evaluation of the evidence for the existence of God. These tools provide a procedure by which the relative weight of the evidence for the existence of God can be measured.

Swinburne also considers other evidence for God's existence. Besides the evidence of the existence of the complex physical universe, there is the evidence of the temporal order of the universe, the evidence of the character of the universe, the evidence of history and miracles, and the evidence of religious experience. With most of this evidence he evaluates the support they give to the theistic hypothesis by applying the tools identified here.[14]

II

Swinburne's method seems particularly appropriate for the evidence he cites. The procedure seems to be an elegant and powerful instrument for answering important questions about the support that evidence gives to a hypothesis. Bayes's theorem presents the particular evidential-support relations in a simple, but informative way, and the application of the

---

[13] *The Existence of God*, p. 132.

[14] His sole exception to this way of calculating evidential support is the evidence of religious experience. He bases the argument from religious experience on the principle of credulity: '(in the absence of special considerations) if it seems (epistemically) to a subject that *x* is present, then probably *x* is present; what one seems to perceive is probably so'. This principle passes the burden of proof to those who doubt the authenticity of religious experience. By the principle of credulity he concludes that religious experience makes probable the existence of God. See *The Existence of God*, pp. 254 ff.

various evaluative criteria provides a definitive method for comparing relevant prior probabilities.

Nevertheless, there are contexts of explanation in which the Bayesian method is not as appropriate. One instance of this is the explanation of evil. The existence of evil is often cited as the most crucial objection to belief in the existence of God. An appropriate response to the problem of evil requires explaining why God allows evil, and it is the evaluation of the power of theistic explanation in this sense which makes difficult the assessment of evil using Bayes's theorem.

Recent literature refers most often to the problem of evil as a logical problem: there is an apparent logical incompatibility between the existence of God and the existence of evil. If God is all-good and all-powerful, it seems reasonable to believe that God would want to eradicate evil and that he is powerful enough to do so. Hence, if God exists, there ought to be no evil. But there is evil. Therefore, there is no all-good, all-powerful God.[15]

Various responses to this objection have been proposed. Among these, probably the most discussed has been the free will defence. Alvin Plantinga, a noted recent proponent of the free will defence, argues that a solution to the logical problem can be had by finding a premiss which, together with the proposition that God exists, entails the possibility of evil. Finding a suitable premiss would demonstrate the consistency of the existence of God with the existence of evil. Plantinga believes that one such premiss is that the world contains creatures with free will. The existence of a good God seems logically consistent with the existence of a universe containing creatures with free will. But it is also logically impossible for God to guarantee that a universe containing creatures with free will would be without evil.[16] It is of course logically conceivable that a universe would contain creatures with free will who would always freely choose the good. But it is not logically possible for God, in creating a universe, to build into the structure of the universe a guarantee that the free creatures would always freely choose the good. If God did build such

---

[15] See J. L. Mackie's seminal essay, 'Evil and Omnipotence', *Mind*, 64 (1955), 200–12.

[16] Alvin Plantinga, *The Nature of Necessity* (Oxford, 1974), 164–74.

guarantees into the fabric of the universe, Plantinga argues, it would be at the cost of significant human freedom.

A resolution of the logical incompatibility must demonstrate how the incompatibility can be resolved, and the free will defence does just that: at least one possible world, namely, one which contains free creatures responsible for the existence of evil, is consistent with the existence of God and entails the possibility of evil. It follows that the existence of evil and the existence of God are logically compatible.

Most often the free will defence is a response to the existence of evil formulated as a logical problem. But evil is sometimes thought to be an evidential problem as well as a logical problem. William Rowe, for example, concludes his discussion of evil this way:

> we must then ask whether it is reasonable to believe that all the instances of profound, seemingly pointless human and animal suffering lead to greater goods. And, if they should somehow all lead to greater goods, is it reasonable to believe that an omnipotent, omniscient being could not have brought about any of those goods without permitting the instances of suffering which supposedly lead to them? When we consider these more general questions in the light of our experience and knowledge of the variety and profusion of human and animal suffering occurring daily in our world, it seems that the answer must be no. . . . In the light of our experience and knowledge of the variety and scale of human and animal suffering in our world, the idea that none of those instances of suffering could have been prevented by an omnipotent being without the loss of a greater good seems an extraordinary, absurd idea, quite beyond our belief.[17]

In Rowe's formulation of the problem of evil, the existence of evil is evidence against the existence of God. As the objection goes, given what we know about the universe with the variety and the scale of evil it contains, belief in God is unreasonable. Of course, it would be unreasonable to believe a proposition the negation of which is entailed by premises known to be true. Such would be the case if we continued to believe in God and believed as well that the existence of God and the existence of evil are logically incompatible. However, Rowe does not argue that belief in God is unreasonable because God's existence is

[17] *Philosophy of Religion* (Encino, Calif., 1978), 89. Cited in Plantinga, 'The Probabilistic Argument', p. 6.

incompatible with the existence of evil. He accepts that the existence of evil does not deductively entail the non-existence of God, but claims that the evil in the universe makes the existence of God unlikely, or improbable.

When the objection from evil is stated in this way, evil is seen as an additional piece of evidence on a par with other facts to be considered in an inductive argument for the existence of God: as the existence of the universe confirms, or makes probable, theism, so evil disconfirms, or makes improbable, theism.

We speak of things like the universe as evidence for God's existence because they are obvious candidates for causal explanation by the action of God. Such evident facts cannot be explained by ordinary scientific explanation; it is possible to see God's intentional action as their cause and to see why we say that the existence of the universe confirms the existence of God. But, with the evidence of evil, the situation is very different. Typically, we do not speak of God as directly causing evil. Since by definition God is perfectly good, we cannot attribute any evil action to him. Hence, it is not because evil is an obvious candidate for explanation by the action of God that we speak of evil as evidence against theism.

The evidential problem of evil originates in the existence of apparently pointless evils, so called gratuitous evil.[18] Evils on a grand scale such as African famines or on a smaller scale such as the death of a young mother occur without any apparent reason. Ordinarily our intuitions about things like this lead us to require someone to prevent the occurrence of evil unless there is sufficient reason not to. Our conception of goodness would be stretched beyond recognition if we attributed goodness to someone who had the power to stop evil but did not. However, this is exactly what we do in God's case: God is all-good and all-powerful, but it seems that he could prevent many, many evils which he does not.

We can illustrate this conflict among our intuitions by way of an analogy. Parents have responsibility for their child's well-being. They must teach their child to live in the world

[18] There is a range of 'problems of evil'. I believe that the problem of gratuitous evil is the only one which is forceful against the theist. Mackie provides a sophisticated description of the problem of gratuitous evil in terms of 'absorption' of evil. See Mackie, *The Miracle of Theism*, pp. 150–6. Cf. M. B. Ahern, *The Problem of Evil* (London, 1971), 1–12.

successfully. Sometimes a loving and good parent will allow his child to fail in some of the child's attempts to accomplish a task. Sometimes these failures bring pain. A child must fall down many times in order to learn to walk. This pain seems warranted because the child learns lessons he would be unable to learn otherwise. However, there are limits to the extent of failure a parent can allow. Pain and suffering on the scale of this example are warranted because of the purpose it serves. Greater pain which would serve no purpose would be completely meaningless. Thus, a good parent would not allow the child to suffer severe injury or to kill himself learning to walk. And so it is with God. God is responsible for his creation. And though it is true that we must fail sometimes in order to learn other things, and, therefore, some amount of suffering and evil are legitimate, there is a limit to the amount of suffering and evil God can allow. Otherwise, it is difficult to attribute goodness to God. The problem of evil is that the evil in the world seems to have greatly exceeded any reasonable limit. Human failures can be disastrous. Humans kill and maim themselves to a degree almost unimaginable. They suffer famine and death from natural occurrences to a similar degree. If there were a God, it seems that he would prevent the extreme examples of evil which the world contains, as a father would prevent his child from suffering severe injury in the process of learning to walk. A good God should have intervened to stop a Hitler or a Stalin and should have caused rain to come to Africa to prevent drought and famine. But the fact is that God did not.

This analogy illustrates the tension which exists among our intuitions about God: God is supposed to be all-powerful and all-good, but he has not prevented evils which, intuitively, it seems that he ought to have prevented if he exists. Swinburne provides a succinct description of the problem:

In our world, the objection goes, things are too serious. There is too much evil which man can do to his fellow, and deterrents of too great seriousness, and so too unpleasant natural evils to give men knowledge thereof. The suffering of children and animals is something which rightly appals us. The game, it may be said, is not worth the candle.[19]

---

[19] *The Existence of God*, p. 219.

We can add two qualifications to this description of the problem of evil. The first is that it does not bring out clearly the difference between a problem about the amount of evil and a problem of the meaninglessness of evil. There can be a great amount of evil, but the evil which exists can be relatively harmless. If we could quantify the amount of evil, we could say that a certain amount is acceptable only if the evil is of a certain sort. So, for example, many instances of immature children learning to avoid fire by burning their hands in a coal-fire flame may be allowable because the pain would have a purpose, but one instance of a person whose life is unwillingly sacrificed at the whim of a despot may not be. It is this qualification which indicates the need for a distinction between the amount of evil in the world and the pointlessness of the evil in the world. Swinburne's illustration in the previous quotation indicates the sort of problem which arises from the meaninglessness of evil in the world. The suffering of children and animals beyond what is necessary for learning to live in this world is the sort of evil which seems pointless and unjustifiable: that sort of evil God ought not to allow.

The second qualification is related to this point about the severity of evil. The problem of evil results from the experience of particular instances of evil. Children suffering from starvation and eventually death in the famine of Ethiopia seems utterly purposeless. We speak, therefore, of the general problem of gratuitous suffering, but it is these individual instances of evil which are problematic. A young mother dies of a mysterious heart illness. We seek some reason why a good God would allow this to occur, a reason why God should not have intervened and prevented this event. The problem here is not about the total amount of evil in the universe, but is about the apparent purposelessness of this mother's death.

It is easy to see why the existence of evil is so often posed as a logical problem. The intuitions about the pointlessness of events in the universe and the goodness of God form a set of prima facie incompatible propositions which must be made consistent. The evidential problem of evil is similar to the logical problem in that the problem is about fit. But it is not an issue of logical fit. The lack of fit involved in the evidential problem of evil is a lack of fit between the existence of evil and the reasons a good God might have for allowing that evil. There is a perceived gap between the existence of a particular instance of evil and the postulated reason for God allowing that evil. Though the purposes and designs God has for history may include the possibility that some evil could occur, the extent of the evil in this world, it is alleged, completely outstrips any supposed justification which may be given for God allowing it: the magnitude of evil in the universe is grossly disproportionate to any reason God may have for permitting it.

The existence of this gap between evil and warrant accounts both for the evidential value of evil and for the typical manner of responding to evil. The unresolved dilemma leads to the rejection of theism: God's existence is judged more improbable the greater the distance between evil and the warrant given for God allowing it. In turn, the response to evil attempts to close the gap, to explain why God allows that particular evil to come about. A response must explain God's action, or lack of action, by presenting a suitable reason for the existence of the evil. This kind of response is traditionally called a theodicy, a vindication of God's goodness.

The need to explain evil by providing a theodicy typifies one sort of theistic explanation. Evil forces us to question God's purposes, and we explain why evil exists by giving good reasons for God's lack of intervention. This is an explanation having to do with reasons for action, or, in the case of evil, for the lack of action, and not with causes of events. Thus, we explain why God allowed Stalin to murder almost indiscriminately by an appeal to God's reasons for creating creatures with free will. Similarly, we explain why God failed to intervene in the processes of nature to prevent famine in Ethiopia by citing God's purposes for creating conditions in which men learn to co-operate with others in order to mature in human love.[20]

With this description of the evidential objection, we can see why Bayes's theorem is not appropriate for assessing the evidence of evil. An instance of evil disconfirms the existence of God whenever we have no apparently plausible reason for God allowing it. The degree of disconfirmation is inversely proportional to how well the postulated reason accounts for evil and,

[20] Traditionally this is called a 'soul-making' theodicy. See John Hick, *Evil and the God of Love* (London, 1966).

at the same time, preserves the goodness of God: the more reprehensible the evil and the less plausible the reason, the more disconfirmed is theism. This pattern of disconfirmation does not fit the Bayesian model.

According to the theorem every proposition has some predictive power in relation to the evidence under consideration. In causal explanations the hypothesis 'predicts' the evidence in an obvious sense: the causal relation can be represented by deductive entailment; so, when it fully explains the evidence, the hypothesis deductively entails the evidence. Therefore, the evidence will be predicted with logical certainty by the hypothesis of a full explanation. But, in an explanation of the sort where theism explains evil, there is no similar predictive power. We can illustrate this by comparing full causal explanation with a full explanation of evil.

By Swinburne's definition, a hypothesis fully explains the evidence when the conjunction of the hypothesis and a statement of the initial conditions deductively entails the evidence.[21] But this definition does not fit the theistic explanation of evil. A statement of God's reasons for allowing a particular evil does not have to entail deductively the existence of the evil in order to explain the evil fully. An example of this is Alvin Plantinga's attempt to give a full explanation of evil with the free will defence.[22] He believes that the existence of creatures with free will, both natural and supernatural, fully warrants the existence of all kinds of evils, both moral and natural. But the free will defence claims that the amount of evil in the world and the particular acts of evil which occur are features of the universe independent of God's will. God creates the universe thereby setting up the context where evil is possible. But evil comes about by the choice of free created agents, not by the action of God. Humans may cause much or little evil, but how much and what evil comes about is due to their choice.

Swinburne offers a slightly different theodicy. He believes that theodicies such as Plantinga's are less likely to be true because the addition of supernatural demonic agents to explain natural evil unnecessarily complicates the hypothesis.[23] For that reason he cites two different considerations for a full

---

[21] See p. 16 above.   [22] *The Nature of Necessity*, pp. 191–2.
[23] *The Existence of God*, pp. 221–2.

explanation of evil: the existence of creatures with free will warrants the existence of moral evil, and natural evil is warranted because it is a necessary condition for the exercise of freedom. But in Swinburne's case, as in Plantinga's, a statement of the theodicy does not deductively entail the existence of any particular evils. He attempts to explain evil fully by giving morally and rationally sufficient reasons for God's lack of intervention. God's failure to prevent a Stalin or a Hitler, and of all those who by volition or negligence co-operated with them, is morally excusable because their free will is of sufficient value to warrant allowing the existence of the evil they brought about.

Theism fully explains evil when the reasons cited by the theodicy completely vindicate God's goodness and show that no actual evil is truly gratuitous. This sort of explanation is inherently less exact than causal explanation. As these examples show, a full explanation of evil cannot be given a value for predictive power as in causal explanation. Consequently, no account of the degree of disconfirmation of theism due to evil can be given using Bayes's theorem since no ascertainable value exists for one of the theorem's essential probabilities.

This conclusion is further corroborated by Swinburne's actual practice in evaluating the evidence for theism. In the first place, he presupposes a non-Bayesian method for assessing the evidence of evil in order to use Bayes's theorem to assess the positive evidence for theism. As noted in the previous section, he seeks to defend a partial explanation rather than a full explanation. Rather than incorporating into the hypothesis of theism sufficient information to entail the existence of the evidence, he includes only the premiss that God exists and not the premiss that God exists and intentionally brought about the existence of the universe.[24] Accordingly, he must turn to more complex considerations in order to assess the predictive power of theism. He needs some criterion for evaluating the predictive power of theism relative to the evidence other than simply the fact that the evidence is entailed by the hypothesis. For this purpose, he appeals to the goodness of the universe as the reason why there is some positive likelihood that the universe would exist if God exists.

[24] *The Existence of God*, p. 69.

Looking at Swinburne's analysis of the cosmological argument, we see where he uses this criterion to determine the predictive power of theism. As we saw in the previous section the explanatory power of a hypothesis is the value of the ratio between the predictive power of the hypothesis and the prior probability of the evidence. With respect to the existence of the universe and the causal explanatory power of theism, the relevant probabilities are the probability that God would create a world like ours and the probability that a universe like ours would exist uncaused. According to Swinburne, the probability that God would create a world like ours is fairly low: God need not have created any world at all.

This lack of predictive power is a standard objection to inductive arguments for God's existence and has been taken by many to be proof that such arguments are impossible.[25] Swinburne accepts the prima facie force of this criticism. But, in fact, he claims, we do have a way to assess the requisite probabilities involved in the argument for God's existence. We know that God is perfectly good. This means that he will always refrain from doing a morally bad action and whatever he does will be morally acceptable. God is incapable of performing certain actions because those actions would be morally bad to do. The range of actions God could not perform would include creating certain worlds which would be so morally bad that a good God could not create them. An example of such a world would be a world where every sentient creature endlessly suffered high levels of pain. That sort of world a good God would be obligated not to allow. In a broad sense, then, we can distinguish worlds which God could allow from those which he could not. On the basis of this criterion, the criterion of the goodness of the world, we can evaluate the predictive power of theism relative to the existence of the universe. Worlds which are on balance good are to be expected if God exists.

In this way Swinburne avoids this objection to inductive arguments for the existence of God: we do in fact have some reason to expect certain worlds rather than others. But his solution reveals that he does not use Bayes's theorem to evaluate the weight of the evidence of evil. It is essential to

[25] Cf. D. H. Mellor, 'God and Probability', *Religious Studies*, 5 (1969), 223–34. See Swinburne's response to Mellor in *The Existence of God*, pp. 112–13.

Swinburne's use of Bayes's theorem with respect to the positive evidence for the existence of God that an affirmative judgement about the moral acceptability of this world is warranted. However, on his account, this prior judgement itself cannot be a Bayesian judgement, that is, it cannot be evaluated by the use of Bayes's theorem. If the argument for the goodness of the universe were assessed using Bayes's theorem, some other criterion would be needed by which the predictive power of the hypothesis could be evaluated. But he has given no other criterion except for the criterion of the goodness of the universe.

A judgement that this universe is the kind of world God could create concerns the very issue in question. It is a judgement that the evil in this world is the sort which God would have reason to allow or bring about. But an objection from evil, formulated as either a logical or an evidential problem, is committed to the negation of this judgement, namely, to the claim that gratuitous evil demonstrates that this world is precisely the sort of world a good God would not allow. Swinburne's use of the criterion of the world's goodness reflects a prior judgement about the evidential significance of the particular kind of evil, a judgement which cannot itself be Bayesian in nature.

His discussion of the problem of the quantity of evil further exemplifies a non-Bayesian assessment of evil. He admits that someone may find his theodicy inadequate. A man, for example, may accept that free will is a good thing and that natural evil is a necessary condition for exercising free will. Nevertheless, he may feel that these reasons do not fully explain God's lack of intervention given extreme cases of evil. They do not completely vindicate God's goodness.

Swinburne addresses this possibility by attending to several further facts about the universe in which we live. First, death cuts off the amount of suffering a single individual must experience, and so there is a limit to suffering built into the universe. Secondly, a limit on the possibility of doing evil—if, for example, God had prevented the occurrence of Stalin's gulags—would similarly limit the extent to which man can exercise his responsibility. If there are fewer contexts which include the possibility of doing evil, there will be fewer contexts in which to exercise mature and responsible freedom. As Swinburne argues,

For the less natural evil, the less knowledge [God] gives to man of how to produce or avoid suffering and disaster, the less opportunity for his exercise of the higher virtues, and the less experience of the harsh possibilities of existence; and the less he allows to men the opportunity to bring about large-scale horrors, the less freedom and responsibility which he gives them.'[26]

In Swinburne's judgement these observations demonstrate that his theodicy leaves no gap that would enable evil to disconfirm theism. Clearly these observations do provide some warrant for God's failure to intervene, and, for that reason, they tend to lessen any discrepancy between the existence of an evil and the reason for allowing that evil. Hence he claims that no good inductive argument against the existence of God can be based on evil. However, this judgement is not the result of a Bayesian assessment, but of a controvertible judgement on the moral acceptability of the theodicy.

III

I have argued in this chapter that Swinburne's treatment of the evidence of evil is an important exception to his Bayesian methodology. The problem of evil provides a clear illustration of evidence which is relevant to theism but which cannot be assessed using Bayes's theorem.

There are two important points to note given this conclusion. The first concerns the general applicability of Bayes's theorem for the assessment of theism. The theorem's failure to measure accurately the weight of the evidence of evil is even more highly significant given the centrality of evil for a case against the existence of God. It suggests strongly that the Bayesian methodology is not appropriate for assessing a case where a wide variety of evidence will be offered in support of or in objection to theism.

The second point is that, though the argument here has used evidence against theism as the example, a similar case could be made using evidence for the existence of God. This will be true whenever the evidence is non-causally explained by the theistic hypothesis. Thus some reasons for God's creating the universe

[26] *The Existence of God*, p. 219.

will provide significantly greater explanatory power than other reasons. For example, the hypothesis that God created the universe because he desired to commune with other free, rational beings explains better the existence of the universe than the hypothesis that God created the universe because he wanted to puzzle finite creatures with the enigma of black holes and the meaning of their existence. A hypothesis which included the former reasons has a concomitantly greater explanatory power and is more probable on the evidence. Another illustration comes from the court room. The explanation of, for example, a bank robbery, will obviously include a reference to an agent. If we know who committed the robbery, we can causally explain the event of the robbery by reference to the agent and his intention to rob the bank. But the explanation is made more forceful if we know the motive behind the bank robbery. Knowing that an agent had to find money to feed his children increases the explanatory power of the hypothesis that he committed the robbery, even if we know already that he did the crime. But this sort of explanatory power is not the kind represented by Bayes's theorem, and its evidential support must be assessed by a non-Bayesian judgement in much the same way as the theistic explanation of evil.

2
EVALUATIVE CRITERIA AND BAYES'S THEOREM

MY analysis to this point has suggested that Bayes's theorem cannot account, in one way or the other, for the evidence of evil or for the explanatory power of theism with respect to evil. But, as we saw, Bayes's theorem incorporates not only the probability of predictive power but also various prior probabilities. These probabilities have no correlate in causality, and, therefore, there is no obvious way, as in the case of predictive power, to calculate their values. For this purpose particular evaluative criteria are required. Swinburne accepts three: fit, scope, and simplicity.

The fact that criteria such as these must be used points to another problem of Bayes's theorem. If differing criteria are used, even granting the logical necessity of epistemic probabilities, the theorem reports conflicting values for the probability of a hypothesis on given evidence. Disputants, by appealing to different evaluative criteria, can agree on the methodology of Bayes's theorem but come to contradictory conclusions. In such a case, the use of Bayes's theorem does not provide a helpful method for assessing the weight of the evidence for a given hypothesis.

In this chapter I shall illustrate this contention by analysing the use of evaluative criteria. I shall argue that conflict over criteria is intractable and shall conclude with further observations about the use of Bayes's theorem in the debate about God.

I

Recall that according to Bayes's theorem a hypothesis can be confirmed by evidence in two ways: if the hypothesis has great predictive power or if the prior probability of the evidence is so low that it would not be expected to exist unless the hypothesis was true. Evaluative criteria come into play in determining the latter of these two considerations. But the criteria are also important in determining the prior probability of the hypothesis. The probability of the hypothesis on given evidence is a function of both the explanatory power of the hypothesis and its prior probability. The evaluative criteria, therefore, are used to determine the prior probability of the hypothesis as well as the prior probability of the evidence.

There are, of course, some cases where the possibilities are well defined and the probabilities can be evaluated in numerical terms. For example, the prior probability of a coin toss landing 'heads' is 1/2. But some criteria must be used in cases where circumstances do not allow a similar well-defined assessment. The application of these criteria allows judgements of comparative probability to be made. Therefore, it is possible to tell which hypothesis is more likely than a given alternative without assigning either hypothesis a specific probability value.[1] Swinburne, for example, often speaks in terms of comparative probabilities. He claims that a personal immaterial being such as God is more simple than a complex physical universe. Neither the existence of God nor the existence of the universe has a specific numerical prior probability, but God is a priori more likely to exist than the universe because God is simpler.

Swinburne gives two arguments for the importance of evaluative criteria, both of which are contained in the following paragraph:

There must be a criterion to choose between the infinite number of theories which are equally successful in predicting the observations already made, if we are ever to be able to make any justified predictions for the future. If we are to predict that the sun will rise tomorrow, we need in order to do so, a theory about how the sun moves. To obtain such a theory we need a criterion for selecting among theories of its motion which have been equally successful in predicting past observations. The history of science reveals that, in the absence of background knowledge, that criterion is basically the criterion of simplicity. It is true that our understanding of when one theory is simpler than another is very much the product of our scientific and mathematical upbringing, but that does not mean that our understanding is in error. We must make the judgements which seem to us

---

[1] Swinburne, *Confirmation Theory*, p. 38.

to be intuitively right. Without using this criterion we could make no progress at all in rational inquiry.[2]

The first argument is a quasi-transcendental one: rational inquiry would be impossible unless there were such evaluative criteria. For any finite phenomenon, an infinite number of possible hypotheses exist which can predict that phenomenon. For example, to explain why the petrol container is missing from the garage, one may postulate the existence of a devilish gremlin, or two gremlins, or three, or four, and so on to infinity. Each hypothesis deductively entails, i.e. predicts, the disappearance of the petrol can. If predictive power is the only criterion by which the probability of a hypothesis is evaluated, each of these hypotheses about gremlins would have a probability equal to the much more probable hypothesis that one's neighbour took the can. As Swinburne sums it up, 'if the sole criterion for judging between theories was their ability to predict, all of these theories would be equally likely to be true, for all of them are equally successful in predicting. The fact that many of the theories are not seriously considered is grounds for supposing that some other criterion [is] at work.'[3]

The second argument is an inductive one: the history of science shows that certain evaluative criteria serve this necessary function. According to Swinburne, scientists from past ages have recognized and utilized three criteria to select a single theory from among many which successfully predict: fit with background knowledge, scope, and simplicity. The more the theoretical or hypothetical entities fit with what is already known about the universe, the more likely the theory is to be true. Further, the more scope a theory has, the less likely the theory is to be true since the more things it applies to the more opportunities it has to go wrong: 'Clearly the more you assert, the more likely you are to make a mistake.'[4]

Thirdly, other things being equal, a simple theory is more likely to be true than a complex one. Swinburne provides numerous examples of the use scientists make of these criteria. Newton's theory about the mechanical relations between material bodies, for example, satisfied them very well. The theory stated four general mathematical laws which governed

---

[2] *The Existence of God*, p. 56.   [3] Ibid.   [4] Ibid. 52.

the mechanical relationships between material bodies. The theory was simple because the laws were few. With only four laws Newton could describe the mechanical relations of all material bodies. And the laws themselves were simple mathematically. The law of gravitation, for example, stated that two material bodies attract each other with forces proportional to the product of their masses and inversely proportional to the square of their distance apart. The theory was of tremendous scope: so there was little background knowledge with which it could or could not fit. But its scope was not so great that the theory covered all relations between material bodies. It did not cover chemical or electrical relations, only the mechanical ones. Therefore, because it satisfied the criteria so well, especially the criterion of simplicity, Newton's theory of mechanics was very likely to be true given the state of knowledge at the time.[5]

For Swinburne's purposes, the criteria of fit and scope have little or no importance. The third criterion, simplicity, is by far the most important. Fit with background knowledge becomes less and less important as the scope of the theory increases. At the most general level there will simply be nothing that is not included within the scope of the theory with which the theory can fit. Theism is this kind of explanation. It explains the entire physical universe and all that it contains. Therefore, there will be no background knowledge with which it fits. And scope has little relevance because of the relative priority of simplicity. Though a theory is less probable the more scope it has, often with scope comes greater simplicity since the restrictions on the scope may be 'arbitrary and complicating'.

Simplicity is important for another reason as well. Swinburne intends to assess the prior probability of theism relative to tautological propositions only.[6] He includes all contingent facts about the universe in the evidence to be explained and leaves as background knowledge nothing but necessary truths. Since the criterion of fit refers only to the contingent facts of the universe, it will be irrelevant for this purpose.[7]

These arguments attempt to narrow the range of relevant criteria to one, namely, simplicity. Using this single criterion,

[5] *The Existence of God*, p. 53–4.   [6] Ibid. 65.
[7] R. G. Swinburne, 'Mackie, Induction and God', *Religious Studies*, 19 (1983), 387.

Swinburne concludes that theism has relatively high prior probability. Theism is a very simple hypothesis for three reasons: first, the hypothesis postulates a very simple kind of explanatory agent (because he is of infinite power, knowledge, and goodness, God is a very simple kind of person); secondly, theism identifies all complete explanation as personal explanation; and thirdly, theism postulates a very natural and intelligible stopping-point for explanation, the choice of an agent. Because it is simple in so many ways, the theistic hypothesis has high prior probability, at least with respect to 'other hypotheses about what there is'.[8]

In contrast to the simplicity of theism, much of the evidence for theism is characterized by extreme complexity. This is the case, in Swinburne's judgement, with the physical universe. He concludes: 'There is a complexity, particularity, and finitude about the universe which cries out for explanation, which God does not have.'[9] Because it is so complex, the universe has very low prior probability, and theism has high explanatory power with respect to it.

II

The logic of Swinburne's use of simplicity is very clear: prior probability is proportional to simplicity and inversely proportional to complexity. Consequently, by applying the criterion of simplicity to the relevant evidence and to the hypothesis of theism, he can determine the relevant probabilities for the use of Bayes's theorem.

But the necessity of using these evaluative criteria reveals a problem with the usefulness of Bayes's theorem. Confirmation theory, as stated earlier, takes the probability values in Bayes's theorem to be logically necessary values relating evidence and conclusion. But though the theorem may reflect accurately the probabilities relative to particular criteria, it reflects the true value of the evidential support of a hypothesis only if the criteria used to assess the probabilities are the correct criteria. However, there is little prior agreement on what constitutes the set of proper criteria. Many diverse criteria can be and are used to assign the initial probabilities. This diversity of opinion

[8] Swinburne, *The Existence of God*, pp. 102–6.   [9] Ibid. 130.

about the correct assessment of prior probabilities circumscribes significantly the use of Bayes's theorem.

The disagreement between Swinburne and Mackie over the existence of God exemplifies this difficulty very well. Mackie approaches confirmation theory in a way similar to Swinburne. He accepts the use of the probability calculus, and for that reason Bayes's theorem, as the logic of confirmation. Thus he accepts in principle Swinburne's method of evaluating the evidence for theism. He states:

There is an important principle which serves as a criterion for a good C-inductive [i.e. a confirming] argument. A hypothesis is confirmed by certain evidence if and only if (apart from or prior to that evidence's being observed) the addition of the hypothesis to the background knowledge or belief makes it more probable that that evidence would occur than it would be in relation to the background knowledge or belief alone. . . . Or, equivalently, a hypothesis is in this sense confirmed by evidence if and only if that evidence would have been more likely to occur if the hypothesis had been true than if it had been false: h is confirmed by e if and only if $P(e/h \;\&\; k) > P(e/{\sim}h \;\&\; k)$. In other words, the evidence raises the probability of the hypothesis if and only if the addition of the hypothesis raises the antecedent probability of the evidence.[10]

Mackie speaks of antecedent probabilities where Swinburne speaks of prior probabilities, but their approach is the same. Confirmation occurs wherever the predictive power of the hypothesis is greater than the prior probability of the evidence (or the antecedent probability of the evidence using Mackie's terms).

The agreement between the two, however, ends with their similar Bayesian methodologies. It is a consequence of Bayes's theorem that, if two alternative hypotheses have similar explanatory power, the evidence confirms to a larger extent the hypothesis with the greater prior probability.[11] Both Mackie and Swinburne give the impression that an assessment of the evidence for theism or atheism is a simple matter of determining the relevant prior probabilities. But though, taken as hypotheses about the nature of the universe, theism and atheism have similar explanatory powers, the assessment of the

[10] *The Miracle of Theism*, p. 96.
[11] See Swinburne, *Confirmation Theory*, pp. 43-7.

prior probabilities of the alternative hypotheses varies tremendously depending on the philosopher. According to Swinburne, theism has high prior probability because of its simplicity, but, according to Mackie, theism is unacceptable because its lack of fit with background knowledge shows that it has very low prior probability. The result of these differences over evaluative criteria is that Bayes's theorem records a vastly different probability for theism on given evidence.

To take the treatment of the cosmological argument as an example, Mackie grants theism a slight power to explain the universe, but argues that it makes no difference since theism has such a low prior probability. He contrasts two ways of construing the theistic hypothesis. First, if the hypothesis of theism is seen as providing an explanation for the entire complex physical universe, the evidence for it must include the universe and all that it contains. Hence, any knowledge of the universe must be excluded from the deliberations about the prior probability of theism. Theism's prior probability on this account must be discerned relative to nothing but logical truth. But Mackie believes this project is incoherent. He objects simply by asking what probability 'could the god-hypothesis have had in relation to these [i.e. logical truths]'.[12] Though this is precisely how Swinburne attempts to determine the prior probability of theism, Mackie uses it as part of a *reductio* argument: the concept of prior probabilities relative only to logical truth is incoherent; if Swinburne meant to assess the prior probability of theism that way, he would be attempting something absurd; therefore, he must intend to assess theism in some other way.

By shifting the discussion away from the probability of theism relative to logical truth, this train of argument directs the argument away from the criterion of simplicity and to the criterion of fit with background knowledge, that is, to what we already know about the universe. This is Mackie's second way of assessing theism. In this sense theism is not a hypothesis postulated to explain the entire universe. Rather, it is a hypothesis about the origin of the universe. On this view theism is one alternative hypothesis which must be assessed relative to background knowledge.

[12] *The Miracle of Theism*, p. 99.

We are now comparing the two rival hypotheses, one that there is no further cause or explanation of the complex universe, the other that there is a god who created it. That there is this universe is common ground, shared by the two hypotheses. Swinburne is arguing that in relation to our background knowledge—which can now include everything that we ordinarily know about ourselves and the world, though it must exclude any specific religious beliefs—it is more likely that there should be an uncaused god who created the world than simply an uncaused universe—that is, a universe with internal causal relationships, but no further cause for its basic laws being as they are or for its being there at all.[13]

This shift is crucial for Mackie's response to Swinburne. The lack of fit with background knowledge is his major objection to theism. First, he believes the use of the concept of 'personal explanation' to describe explanation by the action of God is problematic. Personal explanation depends on the notion of immediately fulfilled intention, something which is to Mackie's mind completely alien to experience. Nothing, he contends, is comparable to this type of causality. Therefore, since theism includes this sort of explanation, the theistic hypothesis is inherently unlikely. Secondly, the idea of a disembodied spirit is also foreign to what we know about the universe, and, similarly, since God is defined as a disembodied spirit, the existence of God is 'intrinsically improbable relative to our background knowledge'.[14] These reasons show that the case for theism on the evidence of the complex universe is very, very low.

The argument from fit stands in stark contrast to Swinburne's use of simplicity. He appeals to simplicity because, in the context of having only logical truth as background knowledge, it is the only possible criterion. He takes this to the extent of dismissing out of hand the very criterion Mackie believes decisive, namely, the disanalogy between human persons and God:

In considering the arguments for the existence of God, we shall begin with a situation of tautological background knowledge, and so the dissimilarities between human persons and the postulated God will not as such effect the prior probability of theism.[15]

---

[13] *The Miracle of Theism*, p. 99.   [14] Ibid. 100.   [15] *The Existence of God*, p. 63 n.

Theism, on Swinburne's account, is very simple, while the universe itself is very complex. Thus, he concludes that the universe is unlikely to come about but for the action of God, and therefore the existence of the universe confirms theism.[16]

The difference between Mackie and Swinburne is not over the nature of Bayes's theorem. Both believe it to represent the epistemic relations of confirmation accurately. The differences lie in the assessment of the initial probabilities necessary to apply the Bayesian functions. Swinburne denies the relevance of the criterion of fit to the hypothesis of theism, while Mackie denies the coherence of the notion of probability relative only to logical truth and therefore denies the decisive importance attributed by Swinburne to simplicity.

The conflict at the level of evaluative criteria demonstrates the limits of the effectiveness of Bayes's theorem. Though both Mackie and Swinburne accept the Bayesian methodology, it does not contribute at all to a common assessment of the evidence. They agree on the nature of confirmation theory, but disagree on the conclusions based on it. It appears, then, that one necessary condition for a common evaluation of evidential support is agreement on the correct criteria. Conversely, when this condition is not satisfied, as in the conflict between Mackie and Swinburne, the theorem will not resolve any substantive questions about the evidential support of a hypothesis. This seems to be the case with the evaluation of the theistic hypothesis.

III

The fact that there are so many criteria a good hypothesis must satisfy increases the difficulty presented by conflicting criteria and makes the conditions for agreement very difficult to achieve. This is again illustrated by Mackie and Swinburne's example, for each has reason to use its own respective criterion.

Fit with background knowledge is recognized by many to be relevant for assessing the worth of a hypothesis. Swinburne admits on the basis of his study of the history of scientific inquiry that often the criterion is used to select a hypothesis,

[16] Ibid. 131.

and others, such as W. H. Newton-Smith, in the philosophy of science agree.[17]

We can illustrate the use of the criterion of fit with the earlier example of the hypothesis about the missing petrol can. There is an infinity of possible explanations, one gremlin, two gremlins, three gremlins, and so on, which have the same predictive power as the hypothesis that one's neighbour took it. One factor which eliminates the hypotheses about gremlins and supports the hypothesis about the neighbour is the criterion of fit with background knowledge. The hypothesis of the neighbour fits with what we know about the world: one's neighbour is a human being who has a house with a lawn that regularly needs mowing; perhaps, the neighbour has a history of borrowing petrol from one's garage, and so on. The hypothesis fits with what is known much better than a hypothesis about gremlins. A gremlin is unlike any known creature and its existence has never been confirmed in actuality; and even if there are gremlins somewhere, they have never been observed in this neighbourhood, and so on. On the basis of this lack of fit with background knowledge of the universe, the various hypotheses about gremlins are unlikely, while on the basis of the fit with background knowledge, the neighbour hypothesis is more likely to be true.[18]

Mackie's stress on fit with background knowledge is consistent with the past practice of scientists and with the conclusions of many philosophers about the set of proper criteria. But Swinburne argues that, though it is in some contexts a proper criterion, in the case of the theistic hypothesis fit is not applicable. The reason is that fit becomes less and less important the greater the scope of the hypothesis. If the scope of a hypothesis spans a set of certain phenomena, then there is no obligation for the hypothesis to fit with what is known about the phenomena; that is, the hypothesis need not fit with the phenomena it is intended to explain. Because theism is a hypothesis about everything other than God, about every contingently existing thing in the universe other than God, there is no obligation for

[17] W. H. Newton-Smith, for example, speaks of inter-theory support and compatibility with well-grounded metaphysical beliefs. These are instances of the criterion of fit. See *The Rationality of Science* (London, 1981), 228–9.

[18] Cf. Swinburne, *The Existence of God*, p. 52.

the theistic hypothesis to fit with our knowledge of what is contained in the universe. Therefore, Swinburne can dismiss, for example, the disanalogy between the person God and mundane human persons.

Swinburne identifies one reason why fit should not be so important. But he draws too strong a conclusion from his argument. He discounts the importance of fit altogether in contexts of hypotheses of great scope and where the prior probability is determined relative to logical truth only. Mackie's insistence on fit is a needed corrective to Swinburne's emphasis on simplicity. He emphasizes fit with background knowledge because he believes that the notion of probabilities relative only to logical truths is incoherent. His judgement about the incoherence of the notion is moot, but he makes a very relevant point by his criticism. It is not clear whether there can be a probability based purely on internal simplicity alone.

Swinburne distinguishes between 'intelligibility' and 'familiarity'. Thus, in a critical response to arguments put forward by Mackie, he states:

The simplicity of a hypothesis is not a matter of its familiarity, whether or not it is exemplified in the world of experience. We could understand and judge to be highly simple the notion of two (logically) distinct variables being linearly related to each other . . ., even if all actual observable variables measured by us were related in more complicated ways.[19]

Swinburne is arguing that the relevant sort of simplicity is related to intelligibility, not familiarity. For something to be recognized as simple, and for that reason to be judged as having high prior probability, it is not necessary to have had any experience of that thing. One can agree that intelligibility can be distinguished from the familiarity of experience and that simple relations and simple things can be judged intelligible without having had any experience of those relations or things. On the other hand it does not seem possible to recognize things as intelligible except in relation to what is known or believed. Intelligibility is not independent of belief. A judgement on the intelligibility of variables related linearly, for example, may be independent of our experience of those particular relations, but

---

[19] 'Mackie, Induction and God', p. 387.

the judgement will not be completely independent of our knowledge of relations in general. Otherwise we could not recognize the relation at all, much less make a judgement about its simplicity. It is odd to say that one could judge as intelligible a proposition which had absolutely no contact with what one knows about the universe. But if this is so, then what is intelligible will not be entirely independent of what is familiar.

Swinburne's own discussion of simplicity bears out this observation. He describes an intelligible entity as 'a kind whose nature and interactions seem natural to us'.[20] But what seems natural is very much a product of our cultural conditioning as any one who has lived in a cross-cultural situation can verify. The barriers between the intelligible and the familiar are simply not that sharp. Swinburne illustrates both the simplicity of naturalness and the fit with background knowledge with examples of the mechanical behaviour of a material body. Compare this statement on intelligibility, 'I am not of course saying that if a theory postulates unobservable entities, it has to postulate ones of an intelligible kind. Clearly good theories often postulate entities which behave in very strange ways',[21] with this one on fit, 'Thus a theory about the behaviour of potassium at low temperatures would fit well with background knowledge in so far as it postulated similar behaviour for potassium to that postulated by other accepted theories for similar substances at low temperatures'.[22] These considerations suggest that a concept is intelligible only against more substantive beliefs than tautologies. In this respect Mackie's insistence on fit with background knowledge is legitimate.

These considerations highlight the significance of background knowledge, something that Swinburne seems to take lightly. He claims that the division between new evidence and background knowledge is an arbitrary one.[23] This allows him

[20] *The Existence of God*, p. 52. In personal conversation Swinburne accepts that his original definition was unfortunately unclear. He wants to distinguish between what is intelligible to us and what fits with background knowledge. In both cases we can speak of something being natural; hence, the confusion. I agree with him that 'fit' in Mackie's sense is not appropriate in the context of theoretical science. But it does seem to me as well that the distinction between intelligibility and fit is sufficiently subtle that my point made here is correct.

[21] Ibid.   [22] Ibid.   [23] Ibid. 16 and 65.

the convenience of separating tautologies from more substantive knowledge and determining the prior probability of theism relative to logical truth only. He chastises Mackie for not taking seriously his intention to start 'without any factual background knowledge . . ., and so to judge the prior possibility of theism solely by a priori considerations, namely in effect simplicity'.[24]

Swinburne does not, however, actually address the important point of Mackie's criticism: there is always some background knowledge to account for, even in a situation where one attempts to determine probabilities relative to logical truth only. Because intelligibility is related to background knowledge, differences in background beliefs will surface regardless of the stipulation against including background belief. And Swinburne's procedure fails to take account of the obvious differences between them on just what the factual background knowledge is. Rightly, given his background belief, Mackie will not entertain the intelligibility of immediately fulfilled intentions, or of the simplicity of such intentions, or of the relatively high prior probability of their existence.

A brief survey of Mackie's published works reveals further profound disagreement with Swinburne about the facts of the universe. They differ not only on the nature of the person, but also on free will, causality, and moral objectivity, differences which are reflected in their differing assessments of the evidence.[25] When Mackie claims that theism does not fit with background knowledge, he assumes a content of background knowledge which entails the very high improbability of theism. He has, for example, no place for any kind of explanation other than scientific explanation. But since theism by definition involves explanation by a person, Mackie's argument is loaded against it.

What counts as background knowledge varies to some degree from person to person and context to context. Therefore, an assessment of intelligibility will vary to some degree from person to person. By stipulating that he will consider the prior

---

[24] 'Mackie, Induction and God', p. 387.
[25] Cf. Mackie, *The Miracle of Theism*, pp. 128–32, on personal explanation, and pp. 166–72, on free will. See his *Ethics: Inventing Right and Wrong* (Harmondsworth, 1977) for his views on the objectivity, or the non-objectivity as the case may be, of morality.

probability of theism relative solely to simplicity, Swinburne attempts to settle substantive questions with insufficient argument. Whether one finds his concept of God intelligible or not is directly related to how one understands the universe. Therefore, even given the coherence of the notion of probability relative to logical truth only, there is reason to believe that background knowledge would be relevant to the assessment of the prior probability of theism. So if, for example, as Mackie believes, the world is uniformly material, a being such as God is bound to be strange and a priori unlikely to exist.

IV

Mackie's use of the criterion of fit appears to be legitimate. But so is Swinburne's use of the criterion of simplicity. Of two alternative hypotheses, equal in all respects except for simplicity, the simpler hypothesis ought to be accepted. Suppose there is a burglary of a local shop. There will be many different hypotheses which could explain who committed the crime: one person, two persons, three, and so on. However, in the absence of any other evidence to indicate that more than one person was involved, the obvious hypothesis to accept is the hypothesis that one person did it.

There are good examples of the proper use of simplicity. However, while few object to the criterion of fit, the criterion of simplicity is controversial. The problem with it is the sheer plurality of meanings. Thus, Swinburne, though clear about his reliance on the concept of simplicity, is not clear on what he means by it. He defines it as follows:

A theory is simple in so far as it postulates few mathematically simple laws holding between entities of an intelligible kind. By a theory postulating 'entities of an intelligible kind', I mean that it postulates entities of a kind whose nature and interactions seem natural to us.[26]

In this definition he describes the simplicity of theories using at least three notions which intuitively count as instances of simplicity. The first has to do with the paucity of laws: simplicity in this sense consists in the fewness of things. The second is an idea of mathematical simplicity. He illustrates this with the

---

[26] *The Existence of God*, p. 52.

example of whole numbers such as 2. Whole numbers of this sort are simpler than numbers closely approximating them such as 1.9999. The third sort of simplicity involves intelligibility or naturalness. Those theoretical entities which are intuitively natural or intelligible are simpler than ones which are less natural and less intelligible.

These variations in the concept of simplicity are included in the definition he gives, but he uses others as well. For example, neatness is considered simple: 'There is a neatness about zero and infinity which particular finite numbers lack. Yet a person with zero capacities would not be a person at all. So in postulating a person with infinite capacity the theist is postulating a person with the simplest kind of capacity possible.'[27] When speaking of the simplicity of God's omnipotence, he states:

It is simpler in just the same way that the hypothesis that some particle has zero mass, or infinite velocity is simpler than the hypothesis that it has a mass of 0.34127 of some unit, or a velocity of 301,000 km/sec. A finite limitation cries out for an explanation of why there is just that particular limit, in a way that limitlessness does not.[28]

He further intimates that simplicity is a matter of fit or coherence: 'Such is the hypothesis of theism. . . . How simple a hypothesis is it? I propose to argue that it is a very simple hypothesis indeed and I shall do this by showing how the divine properties which I have outlined fit together.'[29]

The existence of this diversity is no novelty. Mario Bunge, for example, catalogues no less than twelve uses of the concept in scientific contexts.[30] Furthermore, philosophers of science have attempted at great length to clarify and formalize a notion of simplicity useful in epistemic contexts.[31] The concept's

---

[27] Ibid. 94.　　　　　　　[28] Ibid.　　　　　　　[29] Ibid. 93.

[30] *The Myth of Simplicity* (Englewood Cliffs, NJ, 1963), 66–84.

[31] The classical discussions of simplicity include among others Nelson Goodman, *The Structure of Appearance* (Cambridge, Mass., 1957), 56–90, and Harold Jeffreys, *Scientific Inference*, 3rd edn. (Cambridge, 1973), 34–42. The place of simplicity in confirmation is discussed as well by Stephen Barker in *Induction and Hypothesis* (Ithaca, NY, 1957). Elliott Sober has produced a more recent contribution; see *Simplicity* (Oxford, 1975). Cf. Mary Hesse, 'Simplicity', in Paul Edwards (ed.), *The Encyclopedia of Philosophy*, vii (London, 1967). One is impressed by the artificiality of attempts such as Goodman's to account for our intuitions of simplicity by semantic analysis. It seems obvious that, even if he is successful in accounting for some of our intuitions, a purely semantic approach would not be useful with respect to confirmation of theories.

resistance to analysis has forced many to abandon it in contexts of justification. For this reason simplicity is often considered to be at best a pragmatic criterion rather than one which leads to true or justified hypotheses.[32]

W. H. Newton-Smith, for example, gives two reasons why simplicity is not a proper evaluative criterion. First, simplicity is not objective, but subjective. As he describes it, 'simplicity to a large extent lies in the eyes of the theoretician and not in the theory'.[33] The problem is that no one has formulated a criterion of simplicity successfully which can distinguish between the simplicity of the theory 'as opposed to the language within which the theory is expressed'. Secondly, simplicity does not satisfy the measure of the epistemic value of a criterion, namely, long-term observational success.[34] Science appears to be progressing to a more complex view of the universe rather than to a simpler view. For example, classical Newtonian mechanics are much simpler than contemporary quantum mechanics. Thus simplicity, though frequently used to select between hypotheses, is best taken as a pragmatic criterion rather than as an evaluative one. He concludes as follows: 'This does not mean that we should not continue to opt for simplicity given the choice in contexts in which the notion has hard content. The case for simplicity is pragmatic. It simply is easier to calculate with simpler theories. But there is no reason to see greater relative simplicity of this sort as an indicator of greater verisimilitude.'[35]

Both these criticisms are concerned with the difficulties surrounding the application of simplicity. The first recognizes the lack of consensus on just what simplicity is and the problems inherent in the attempt to analyse it. The second compares the

---

[32] See Bunge, *The Myth of Simplicity*, pp. 90–7. Also see Rom Harré, *The Anticipation of Nature* (London, 1965), 105, Bas C. van Fraassen, *The Scientific Image* (Oxford, 1980), 87 f., and Newton-Smith, *The Rationality of Science*, pp. 230–2.

[33] *The Rationality of Science*, p. 231.   [34] Ibid. 230.

[35] Ibid. 231. Newton-Smith uses the concept of verisimilitude, which he roughly describes as 'approximate truth'. The problem is that we cannot explain the activity of science as a rational activity in search of truth when we have no way to recognize truth when we find it. This is especially important in explaining the progress of science. The idea is that scientific theories are not 'true', but 'approximately true'. Progress in science is the progressive increase in approximate truth. His discussion of simplicity is in the context of increasing verisimilitude rather than truth, but for our purpose the distinction is irrelevant.

claims of simplicity with the apparent progress of science. Science demonstrates that the world is not a simple place. But though these criticisms identify important issues concerning simplicity, they do not give reason to doubt that its use as an evaluative criterion is correct. The reason for this has to do with the nature of the concept itself.

Often the philosophical analysis of a concept is taken to be an inductive procedure. We analyse a concept by identifying its clear instances and deriving from them a generalization which preserves the essential elements while eliminating the inessential. The resulting formal concept should be clear in its meaning and ought to be useful in selecting from borderline cases those which do and those which do not fall within the bounds of the concept. Newton-Smith's first criticism depends on taking simplicity to be a formal concept of this kind. He is able to cite examples where the simplicity of the hypothesis is unclear: the simplicity appears to be the result of the language with which it is expressed rather than of anything essential to the theory itself. This is especially evident in the attempts to formalize a criterion of simplicity in mathematically expressed theories.[36] But in contrast to those examples there are other examples where the distinction is very precise. In the example of the burglary above, there is no problem identifying what it is about the one-person theory which makes it simpler than the multiple-person theory. The problem is that no single use of simplicity is definitive, and some purported instances of simplicity may fall prey to Newton-Smith's objection.

Any particular attempt at analysis runs headlong into the conflicting but equally intuitively obvious uses. Newton-Smith recognises this fact and from it concludes that the concept must be a subjective and pragmatic one. His mistake is to believe that there is, or ought to be, a single meaning of concepts such as simplicity. The attempts to analyse simplicity demonstrate that it has no single, or essential, meaning. The fundamental conflict could be resolved only by choosing some particular instance of simplicity as prior, but this would violate the inductive character of the analysis.

---

[36] Cf. Jeffreys' proposal in *Scientific Inference*, p. 38. Hesse summarizes the problems inherent in the formulation of a criterion of simplicity along mathematical lines. See 'Simplicity', p. 446.

Concepts such as simplicity are 'systematically ambiguous'. Wittgenstein introduced the idea of family resemblance, which is appropriate in this context.[37] Simplicity is not a concept which can be analysed into its constituent parts, some of which are essential and some of which are not. Rather, it identifies a range of concepts which involves a 'complicated network of similarities. . . . Such a concept resembles a long rope twisted together out of many shorter fibres. It is held together by the overlapping of many similarities, similarities "in the large" and "in the small".'[38] This overlap produces the family of concepts which in the present context we call simplicity.

If ambiguity implies subjectivity, we run the risk of eliminating all evaluative criteria. Newton-Smith includes among others criteria such as fertility, smoothness, and compatibility with well-grounded metaphysical beliefs in his list of good-making features of a scientific theory.[39] These criteria, however, exhibit no more precision than does simplicity.

V

The conclusion of these past few sections has been that both simplicity and fit are good criteria. Hence, the argument over the existence of God provides a very good illustration of the problem of conflicting criteria. The methods of Mackie and Swinburne are Bayesian, but they disagree over the relevant criteria for assessing the prior probabilities, and, therefore, they come to widely diverging views on those probabilities.

The problem about simplicity is not so much the ambiguity of the concept as the conflict between its various applications. The various uses compete for priority, and no essential concept of simplicity exists to adjudicate between them. Anthony O'Hear, for example, agrees that theism may be simpler than atheism in some respects. But it is equally obvious that

---

[37] See *Philosophical Investigations*, ed. by G. E. M. Anscombe and R. Rhees, trans. G. E. M. Anscombe, 2nd ed. (Oxford, 1958), paras. 65–71.

[38] G. P. Baker and P. M. S. Hacker, *Wittgenstein: Meaning and Understanding*, i (Oxford, 1980), 191.

[39] *The Rationality of Science*, pp. 226–32.

atheism is simpler than theism in some other respects. A deity and a universe is more complex than simply a universe alone.[40]

Nor is the problem of diverse criteria confined to the debate over the existence of God. In recent philosophy of science, for example, the place of non-empirical criteria in the acceptance of particular scientific hypotheses has received a lot of attention.[41] There are many different concerns in addition to empirical adequacy which come to bear on the acceptance of a scientific theory. As noted above, Newton-Smith identifies, besides simplicity, several other criteria such as smoothness and fertility which make a theory a good one. Others may accept a slightly different set of criteria. Paul R. Thagard, for example, believes the important criteria are simplicity, consilience, and analogy.[42]

Some of these criteria are analogous to Swinburne's use of simplicity. Take, for example, the notion of consilience. Consilience is a term, as Thagard describes it, designed to describe 'how much a theory explains. . . . Roughly, a theory is said to be consilient if it explains at least two classes of facts.'[43] Consilience is the explanation of two distinct classes of facts by another. But this is another way of saying that the explanatory theory simplifies. Swinburne cites the power of theism to reduce classes of explanation as one aspect of its simplicity: 'Theism is also intrinsically very simple in a further respect. According to the theist, all explanation is reducible to personal explanation, in the sense that the operation and causal efficacy of the factors cited in scientific explanation is always explicable by the action of a person.'[44] Others are analogous to Mackie's use of fit. For example, Newton-Smith's suggestion that

---

[40] This problem pops up as well in other contexts. In respect to the mind–body problem, Michael Levin distinguishes between ideological simplicity and ontological simplicity, i.e. simplicity of predicates and simplicity of things. He argues that dualism unnecessarily complicates the world's ontology. See *Metaphysics and the Mind–Body Problem* (Oxford, 1979), 88–91.

[41] The seminal essay is Thomas Kuhn, *The Structure of Scientific Revolutions*, 2nd edn. (Chicago, 1970). Kuhn extends somewhat his thesis in a volume of essays *The Essential Tension* (Chicago, 1977). On the subject of the objectivity and rationality of scientific progress, see especially the essay entitled 'Objectivity, Value Judgment, and Theory Choice'. For a more recent volume discussing Kuhnian philosophy of science, see Gary Gutting (ed.), *Paradigms and Revolutions* (Notre Dame, Ind., 1980).

[42] Paul R. Thagard, 'The Best Explanation: Criteria for Theory Choice', *Journal of Philosophy*, 75 (1978), 76–92.

[43] Ibid. 79.   [44] *The Existence of God*, p. 102.

inter-theory support and compatibility with well-grounded
metaphysical beliefs are instances of fit and Thagard's concept
of analogy emphasize the need to draw upon concepts in background knowledge for new concepts in scientific theory-
building. The need for analogies makes fit with background
knowledge important for accepting a new hypothesis. But,
though there are similarities amongst some of the postulated
criteria, the fact remains that, as both the philosophy of religion
and the philosophy of science exemplify, the diversity of criteria
is the rule rather than the exception.

The existence of such diversity confirms the observation
made in the introduction to this chapter regarding the use of
Bayes's theorem. Though any particular judgement about evidential support may conform to it, the theorem does not provide any method for determining which, if either, of two contradictory judgements is correct. This is illustrated by Mackie
and Swinburne's dispute. In spite of the fact that both believe
their respective conclusions are validated by Bayes's theorem,
their dispute cannot be mediated by using the theorem.

The conflict could be resolved if a more basic criterion were
found which would mediate between the conflicting criteria.
Agreement over the relevant criteria for using Bayes's theorem
is in principle possible. This is witnessed most obviously by
examples from the natural sciences, where certain practices
such as the experimental corroboration of hypotheses hold pre-
eminence. But this fact confirms the centrality of agreement for
using Bayes's theorem and shows also why the theorem is
unhelpful in contexts of disagreement. If a most basic criterion
existed—for example, some a priori logical principle—it might
be the case that, by successive applications of the basic
criterion, some agreement could be reached concerning the less
fundamental criteria. However, no most basic criterion of this
kind exists. This is evidenced both by the fact that no such
criterion is presently available—if there were, there would be
no conflicts—and also by a more general consideration about
the nature of criteria, a consideration illustrated by Newton-
Smith's second objection to the use of simplicity as an evaluative criterion.

According to Newton-Smith, the progress of science has not
borne out the assumption that reality is simpler rather than

more complex. Therefore, simplicity may not be taken as a criterion of truth (or verisimilitude), though it may be taken as having purely pragmatic value.

If, however, simplicity is, as we have suggested, a family concept, then any general argument of this kind against simplicity will be problematic. The error will lie in attacking a particular view of simplicity as if it must apply to all uses of the concept. Given the systematic ambiguity of simplicity, some uses of the concept will obviously be irrelevant in particular evaluative contexts, and, of those uses which are relevant, some will be better than others. The simplicity relevant in the context of a hypothesis about the provenance of a letter, for example, may not be the same sort of simplicity relevant in the context of theorizing in the physical sciences. Therefore, the force of Newton-Smith's criticism is weakened by its excessive generality.

But this argument against simplicity fails for a second reason. Newton-Smith commits himself unjustifiably to a particular position about the relation between simplicity and reality. His argument contains two separate premisses. First, if simplicity is a true criterion, it will be so because there is a direct correspondence between simplicity and reality. The efficacy of the criterion of simplicity is due to its description of reality. Since the aim of a theory is to describe reality accurately, a theory is more likely to do so irrespective of other considerations in so far as it reflects the simplicity of reality. The second premiss follows from the first. If simplicity is a true criterion, then science ought to be revealing progressively a simpler universe. Together these two premisses constitute the heart of his argument: if simplicity is efficacious because it describes reality, this ought to be vindicated by the progress of science; it is not vindicated because science reveals a more complex universe rather than a simpler one; therefore, as Newton-Smith concludes, the criterion is not a true evaluative criterion.

We can agree that Newton-Smith's own consideration tells strongly against simplicity used to describe the universe. Our best scientific theories are presently moving toward a more complex view of the universe rather than a simpler one. But the significance of this fact for the criterion of simplicity is lessened if we take into account that we do not know why particular evaluative criteria are successful. In order to know why evaluative criteria succeed, we would need to know what the universe was like apart from the use of the criteria. However, we do not have such privileged access to the universe, and we cannot determine what the universe is like apart from the use of our very best criteria (which includes the criterion of simplicity).[45] Thus arguments such as Newton-Smith's which presume some specific relation err because they assume that the evaluative criteria must relate to reality in a specific way.

If it were efficacious as a criterion because of some indirect relation to reality, simplicity could be a true evaluative criterion, without there being long-term observational success of the kind Newton-Smith demands. This is suggested by Swinburne's insistence that simplicity is important, 'other things being equal'.[46] Rather than there being a correspondence between simplicity and ultimate reality, simplicity finds its relevance in relation to other criteria. Considerations such as fit and predictiveness serve as primary criteria, while simplicity finds its relevance in conjunction with them. Simple theories are more likely to satisfy these other criteria than complex ones. In this way simplicity is related to the justification of a hypothesis in an indirect but authentically evaluative way.

This argument shows why there can be no most basic criterion for selecting between less fundamental criteria. In order to have any such criterion, we would need to have some privileged access to reality. We would need to know by some means other than by our normal evaluative criteria which criterion was correct. But this privileged access we do not have. Any selection from among the diversity of criteria must be done on the basis of the application of the same criteria, and, as in the argument about the existence of God or in the selection of scientific hypotheses, diversity is the rule rather than the exception.

If there can be no most basic criterion for selecting less basic criteria, then the only way to determine them is through argument. Swinburne, for example, uses an inductive argument from history as well as more conceptual considerations in his

---

[45] Cf. Richard Rorty, *Philosophy and the Mirror of Nature* (Oxford, 1980), pt. 2.
[46] Cf. *The Existence of God*, p. 52.

argument for simplicity. But Bayes's theorem will not be applicable to these arguments. The application of the theorem to decide which criteria are correct would require using the very criteria which are in question. In other words, Bayes's theorem, because its use depends on the application of evaluative criteria, cannot help determine which criteria are correct without begging the question. For that reason the theorem will be unhelpful in selecting the set of correct criteria.

The most we can say is that Bayes's theorem, as the example of the argument between Mackie and Swinburne illustrates, represents the evidential support relative to particular criteria. Only when the criteria are the correct criteria will the theorem represent the actual evidential support for a hypothesis, but what the correct criteria are will be the locus of profound disagreement.

These first two chapters constitute both 'in-principle' and 'in-practice' arguments against the use of Bayes's theorem: in principle because the theorem does not seem capable of recording the evidential value of evidence such as evil, in practice because, though nothing excludes the possibility of agreement about criteria, the existing state of affairs in the debate over the existence of God as illustrated by Swinburne and Mackie provides little reason to believe that sufficient agreement for the use of Bayes's theorem will come about.

From these considerations it follows that the use of Bayes's theorem is not a completely satisfactory method for assessing the evidential support for theism. And since he uses Bayes's theorem as the principal tool to assess the evidence for the existence of God, Swinburne is less likely to present an adequate account of the case for theism: either he will fail to account for some important evidence such as evil or he will draw unwarranted conclusions based on too narrow a base of evaluative criteria.

If we are to evaluate the evidential support for the existence of God satisfactorily, we need a way to account for all kinds of evidence and to evaluate hypotheses in the context of disagreement about evaluative criteria. In the next chapter I shall discuss this project.

3

INFORMAL REASONING AND RELIGIOUS BELIEF (1)

WE have, up to this point, discussed particular problems associated with the approach Swinburne adopts in his argument for the existence of God. We saw, in the first place, that his methodology is inadequate for evaluating the explanatory power of theism. Bayes's theorem cannot account for the different kinds of evidence which are essential for assessing the evidential support for theism, nor can the theorem be readily applied to explanations which are not predictive in the way most scientific hypotheses are. A second problem arises from the use of evaluative criteria such as simplicity. Though the use of simplicity is warranted, there are several relevant senses of simplicity and various kinds of relevant evaluative criteria which together lead to conflicting judgements if applied to the same case. The resulting conflicts in turn are not amenable to a Bayesian resolution, and thus they constitute a practical limit to the usefulness of the theorem.

This leaves unresolved the question of how to evaluate the case for theism. Given the inconclusiveness of the traditional deductive arguments, an inductive approach is the obvious alternative. But if Bayes's theorem represents the logic of induction, even induction will be problematic in this context. In this chapter I want to discuss one particular suggestion for resolving the problem. Basil Mitchell argues that justifying large-scale hypotheses such as theism requires a less formal method than the methods required either for deductive justification or for inductive justification using probability theory. I shall argue that, given a certain interpretation, his fundamental suggestion is sound and that it offers a fruitful reading of the theistic arguments.

I

According to Mitchell the apparent deficiencies of the traditional deductive and inductive arguments can be surmounted if the theistic argument is construed differently:

What has been taken to be a series of failures when treated as attempts at purely deductive or inductive argument could well be better understood as contributions to a cumulative case. On this view the theist is urging that traditional Christian theism makes better sense of all the evidence available than does any alternative on offer, and the atheist is contesting the claim.[1]

In this assertion Mitchell makes two separate claims which are not always distinguished. The first of these has to do with the nature of explanation, the second has to do with the logic of the argument. The notion of theism as an explanatory hypothesis will be discussed in Chapter 5. Here I wish to concentrate upon the second aspect of the suggestion. In the above quotation Mitchell speaks of a 'cumulative case' which is not of the ordinary deductive or inductive kind.

In clarifying this kind of reasoning he makes use of some observations made by John Wisdom. Wisdom writes: 'The process of argument is not a chain of demonstrative reasoning. It is a presenting and representing of those features of a case which severally cooperate in favour of the conclusion.'[2] Mitchell sees this as an apt description of the way evidence is presented in support of a conclusion in a cumulative-case argument. In a deductive argument one states the relevant premises and identifies the relevant formal inference patterns which authorize the conclusion. In an inductive argument such as Swinburne's, evidence is presented which confers a degree of probability that can be represented by the axioms of the probability calculus. Mitchell believes that acceptable reasoning does not always follow these two patterns. In a cumulative argument, as he understands it, one identifies a set of considerations that together can be said to support a conclusion.

The two aspects of Mitchell's argument, the concept of explanation and the logic of a cumulative argument, are often not

---

[1] *The Justification of Religious Belief*, pp. 40–1.
[2] John Wisdom, 'Gods', *Proceedings of the Aristotelian Society* (1944–5), cited in Mitchell, *The Justification of Religious Belief*, p. 45.

separated. They can be confused because there is a superficial parallel between the idea of a cumulative case as an argument which is based on the explanation of several different strands of evidence and the idea of a cumulative case as a description of the logic of the argument. In the first sense the case for theism is cumulative because it explains many different kinds of evidence, for example, the existence of the world and the existence of miracles. Inductive arguments such as Swinburne's are also cumulative-case arguments in this sense. In the second instance the cumulative case for theism refers to the way in which the weight of the evidence for theism is assessed. The concern is with the type of reasoning evident in a judgement of this sort. The contrast is with deductive proof or inductive probability or, as Wisdom states it, 'a chain of demonstrative reasoning'. Here the sense of cumulative-case reasoning contrasts with Swinburne's approach.[3] Because Mitchell does not clearly distinguish these two senses of cumulative case, his suggestions are liable to be confusing.

In the main Mitchell's goal is to illustrate this sort of reasoning and to argue that the case for theism is an instance of it. However, he does not spell out in much detail what the logic of the cumulative case is. Though he supplies numerous examples of arguments that illustrate his thesis, he fails to provide a detailed analysis of cumulative-case argumentation taken as an independent mode of reasoning. For this reason he leaves great latitude in interpreting and evaluating his argument.[4] In the following sections I shall provide an interpretation of Mitchell which remedies some of the incompleteness of his own exposition. In particular I shall argue that there is a specific logic of cumulative-case reasoning and that a proper understanding of that logic makes perspicuous the centrality of personal judgement.

II

Whereas the concept of a cumulative case refers to the method of presenting evidence in support of a conclusion, the concept of

[3] Cf. Swinburne, *The Existence of God*, pp. 13 f.

[4] Cf. e.g. Michael Durrant, rev. of *The Justification of Religious Belief*, *Religious Studies*, 10 (1974), 233–6, Roderick Sykes, 'Soft Rationalism', *International Journal for Philosophy of Religion*, 8 (1977), 51–66, and William J. Abraham, *An Introduction to Philosophy of Religion* (Englewood Cliffs, NJ, 1985), ch. 9.

informal reasoning refers to the logic which supports a cumulative case. J. R. Lucas provides an illustration which may help to clarify the idea of informal reasoning. He calls it 'the argument of the judge'.[5] Consider a judge making a decision concerning the applicability of a particular law to a given case. The law may clearly apply to the case at hand; if so, the judge subsumes the case under the proper law. For example, driving a car to the supermarket without using the seat-belt clearly violates the law requiring the use of seat-belts by the driver and front-seat passenger in private cars. But sometimes the applicability of the law is unclear. For example, suppose a young father-to-be fails to fasten his seat-belt while frantically driving his wife to the hospital. Is the legislation intended to apply to this sort of emergency situation? In situations where circumstances are extenuating, there may be question whether the seat-belt law applies at all. Guidelines for decision-making in this situation may exist, but the fact is that the law will not determine the specific decision of the judge. Here the judge must make an 'educated' judgement on the proper application of the law.

The judge's decision in the context of the imprecision of the law is an instance of informal reasoning. His final verdict is not based on reasoning which conforms to a set of specific rules that make the conclusion acceptable. In the example of the judge, no specific rule, in this case, no specific law, determines what decision he will make.

Assertions based on informal reasoning are not arbitrary. They are not settled, so to speak, by the flip of a coin. Though the reasoning is not governed by specific rules, not everything counts as an instance of acceptable reasoning. The legal system recognizes this and prohibits arbitrary decisions in situations of ambiguity. The judge's decision must be rationally defensible or it will be overturned upon appeal. It can be assessed as a good or a bad verdict, in spite of the fact that it is not the consequence of the application of specific laws governing such decisions. In the law court good judgement is discernibly different from bad judgement; yet neither is simply the application of a law. Thus, Lucas concludes:

---

[5] 'The Lesbian Rule', *Philosophy*, 30 (1955), 200.

good judges decide their cases neither according to any rigid rule, good or bad, nor randomly, that is according to no-rule. There is thus not an exhaustive disjunction between being in accordance with some definite rule and being completely unruly, between the conclusively justified and quite unjustified. Judicial decisions are not in accordance with inescapable reasons, but nonetheless are capable of being reasonable and right.[6]

This illustration helpfully illuminates the difference between formal and informal modes of reasoning. The difference has to do with the particular conventions governing the inference. In formal reasoning the conventions are determinate: premisses must be stated, and conclusions are derived by formal inference patterns from those premisses. In the example of the judge it follows deductively from the conjunction of the premiss stating that the act of driving was without a fastened seat-belt and the relevant law that an offence was committed. Therefore, if the case is straightforward, the judge can subsume the illegal act under the relevant law and impose a fine. Here the judge's decision follows the formal deductive pattern. In informal reasoning the conventions of inference are not so rigidly defined, and conclusions resulting from informal reasoning are not justified in the light of applying determinate inference patterns. The judge, in the context of the ambiguity, must make a decision which does not follow a formal pattern since the statute does not directly speak of the case at hand.

The fact that we recognize the rationality of the judge's decisions lends weight to the assertion that informal reasoning is an alternative to the traditional deductive and inductive modes. There simply is no set of conventions which govern any and every proper inference; nor are rational beliefs in every case the consequence of the purely technical application of the conventional rules such as the patterns of deductive inference. Rather, there is an essential logical difference between informal and formal modes of reasoning, and, in informal reasoning at least, there is an inescapable and necessary element of evaluative judgement.

Lucas's discussion of the logic of informal reasoning revolves around understanding the logic of singular reasons in moral and historical reasoning. The problem he addresses is whether

---

[6] 'Lesbian Rule', p. 200.

there can be rational discourse in morals or history if there are no determinate rules which guide the discourse. He comments: 'The problem with which I wish to deal . . . is the problem of singular reasons in the humanities, whether they exist, or rather, whether they *can* exist: for it would seem that the word "reason" carried with it some idea of generality, so that the phrase "singular reason" was a contradiction in terms, a specification which could never be fulfilled.'[7]

The apparent tension, as Lucas sees it, is between the implied generality of a reason and the fact that there is only one instance of the reason. In the case of the judge, his reasons for preferring one ruling over another are singular ones. In other disciplines such as history, the prevalence of singular reasons is due to the unique circumstances of historical events. Thus, for example, the events and affairs which led to the rise of Napoleon were unique to that epoch and explain only the rise of Napoleon, not the rise of Caesar.

The problem with singular reasons is that good reasoning is often associated with having a definite decision procedure constituted by reaching a conclusion through an appeal to a general rule. This kind of decision procedure is associated with the Hempelian account of scientific method.[8] Science, Hempel claims, seeks universal generalizations in the form of nomological propositions under which experiential data can be classified. A scientific law governing a class of phenomena can be used to predict the outcomes of experiments involving that class of things. The experiment can therefore be used as a decision procedure to test the scientific law. It is this generality which singular reasons lack.

As Lucas argues, however, this tension is only apparent since, as the case of the judge shows, not all good reasoning involves a definite decision procedure. He comments:

The thesis is . . . to be rejected on more central grounds, that it is based upon a false extension of the idea of a decision procedure, and that it leads to impossible results. The thesis can be restated as the claim that value words carry with them an undertaking to justify if required. Words like 'true', 'right', 'valid', 'cause', 'consequence', would all mean 'conclusively provable', and might legitimately be

[7] Ibid. 195.
[8] See *Philosophy of Natural Science* (Englewood Cliffs, NJ, 1966), 47–69.

used only if there is a decision procedure available, whether of observation or scientific experiment, truth table analysis, or a chain of incontestable deductive steps. In moral contexts on this hypothesis, a man could properly use the words 'ought', 'might', or 'should', only if there were some accepted book of rules, a decalogue or a code Napoleon, by means of which he could conclusively establish his correctitude. But it is not so: the thesis fails because we have, and must have, uses for words like 'right' when there are no inescapable or publicly demonstrable justifications to support it.[9]

The argument of the judge, as well as countless other examples, illustrates a rational and justified conclusion which does not come about by following a definite rule-based decision procedure.

III

In his discussion of a cumulative case Mitchell gives an argument which is in some respects similar to the argument of the judge given above. He makes a different point, however. He seeks to exemplify the necessary reliance of reasoning on a capacity for judgement. There are two reasons why all reasoning cannot be a matter of following a set of specific conventions, and both involve the existence of a vicious infinite regress. In the first instance, if all reasoning involved following certain conventions, there is a problem in deciding what the correct conventions are. Clearly, if a person is free to select the proper convention as he wills, that is 'the end of rationality'. But if he is not, he must show that the conventions he uses are in fact the correct ones. And this involves at some point illustrating that these conventions are the ones which are in fact used by good reasoners. But in any examination of the actual reasoning of persons, as illustrated by the argument of the judge, cases exist where no specific convention clearly applies. Thus, some judgement must be made about these recalcitrant examples. Mitchell notes that there are three possibilities (Mitchell uses the term 'rule' where I use the term 'convention', but the idea is the same):

[9] 'Lesbian Rule', pp. 199–200.

(a) the cases can be made to fit without distortion; (b) the cases are not genuine examples of reasoning; (c) the rules have not been correctly specified. To decide between these possibilities requires thought. If this exercise of thought has itself to be rule-governed, the question can in turn be raised whether these rules have been correctly specified, and so on *ad infinitum*.[10]

The second reason why all reasoning cannot be a matter of following specific conventions follows from the first: even if the conventions have been correctly specified, there are cases where it is not obvious which convention to apply. These cases, again, require some judgement with respect to which convention applies. 'Here too,' Mitchell asserts, 'a regress seems inevitable unless we recognise a capacity for judgement, which does not itself consist in the following of rules.'[11]

It is essential to see these arguments in their context. Mitchell is rejecting the claim that rationality is a function of applying a set of specified conventions leading to justified conclusions. By judgement in this context he refers to the act of assessing singular reasons in the sense which we saw in Lucas's example above. The problem of the infinite regress is endemic to the claim that all reasoning must follow a certain pattern, namely, subsuming premises and conclusions under a set of specific inference rules. It is only when this is made a requirement for rationality that the infinite regress is an issue, for, as Mitchell and Lucas demonstrate, in certain contexts there can be no specified conventions by which the argument is assessed.

Mitchell's proposals clarify further the idea of informal reasoning. The argument of the judge illustrates informal reasoning in practice, while Mitchell's claims show up the centrality of judgement to the process of informal reasoning. It may be felt, however, that the necessity of making a judgement is the very thing which is problematic. How can judgements be assessed if it is not by the application of conventions? The argument of the judge illustrated that the required judgement is not simply a matter of arbitrary choice. Judgements can be good ones or bad ones as the judge's verdict exemplifies. The task is to understand how judgements can be assessed.

Judgements can be assessed because there is a condition of rationality which in effect circumscribes the parameters of

[10] *The Justification of Religious Belief*, p. 89.   [11] Ibid.

informal reasoning. Lucas identifies this condition as the requirement of consistency. That is to say, the weight of similar arguments must, on account of the similarity, be similarly assessed; or, alternatively, similar reasons must be afforded similar weight. He writes:

in the humanities . . ., it has to be possible, given a situation or given an argument, to find that any other situation or any other argument sufficiently closely resembling or sufficiently close to the given one has a similar response or a similar value to that of the given situation or argument, provided always that the standard of closeness of resemblance or closeness for the response or the value of the function is to be given first.[12]

The criterion of consistency guides informal deliberations, but is not so stringent as to outlaw informal reasoning from the start.

The requirement of consistency shifts the burden of proof. Formal reasoning requires that a conclusion be justified by applying a general convention. The opponent in an argument must only show how in the particular argument the general convention is not satisfied; whereupon the argument fails. This is an argument in which decisive counter-examples conclusively disprove the proposition under discussion. The argument can of course be amended to overcome the counter-example, but in general falsification is effected by showing how the convention is not satisfied. Thus, the burden of proof in a formal argument falls on the proponent: as long as the opponent can show how the convention fails to cover the proposed conclusion, the opponent is within his rights to remain unconvinced.

In contrast, because there is no set of specific conventions which justifies informal reasoning, the consistency condition simply requires that, for any rule deployed, that rule be used consistently. In other words, consistency requires that similar arguments must be similarly assessed (as a good one or as a bad one). Here the burden of proof is on the opponent. He must demonstrate where the inconsistency lies. In an actual argument this will take the form of providing counter-arguments or counter-examples which will show not that the argument does

[12] 'Lesbian Rule', p. 210.

not fall under a specific convention, but that there is an important difference which calls for a different assessment. He will draw attention to a distinction from or a similarity to another argument which will suggest the need for a different assessment. The burden of proof is still on the opponent, not the proponent, to show the relevant difference. The proponent need only show how the point of dissimilarity is irrelevant or how it is truly not a point of real dissimilarity.[13]

The importance of this for understanding informal reasoning is that informal arguments are concerned with distinctions and differences rather than with specific conventions and subsumption of arguments under those conventions.[14] The criterion of consistency forces one to apply similar reasoning in cases of sufficient similarity. Showing a difference challenges the consistency with which a person argues, but it does not conclusively disprove the conclusion, for it is always open to him to show how the alleged difference is irrelevant. With formal reasoning, by contrast, the object is to derive a particular judgement from a more general rule or law. The challenge here is to make sure that the assertion conforms to the proper conventions. The burden is on the one who claims that the assertion does fall under the current convention to show that it does; and an opponent has but to give a counter-example and the assertion itself loses its weight.

The requirement of consistency reflects the fact that informal reasoning, though not convention governed as is formal reasoning, is none the less not arbitrary. Lucas distinguishes two senses of the word 'some' with respect to reasoning. The term can refer to a specific and definite convention which can be cited under questioning, i.e. to some particular convention. Or it can mean not-none, which is to say that there is a rule, though one which cannot be cited beforehand.[15] Informal reasoning requires that, whatever rules, or reasons, are used, they are used consistently. The idea of a singular reason, most evident in informal reasoning, does not mean that there is no rule, but only that the rules used are revealed in the argument itself and cannot be specified beforehand as conventions.[16]

---

[13] Ibid. 205.   [14] Ibid. 204.

[15] Ibid. 205. Lucas admits two other constraints on informal reasoning: rules of relevance and universalizability. See *The Freedom of the Will* (Oxford, 1970), 39.

[16] Lucas, *The Freedom of the Will*, p. 39.

Lucas illustrates the distinction between having a specific convention and having a non-specified rule by drawing on material from historical research. Though historians rightly refuse to speak of general laws of history, they are willing to speak of similarities and to 'accept the liability of demonstrating how apparently similar situations which were not followed by similar results were in fact different in some significant circumstance, which would explain the dissimilarity of consequence'.[17] This is an instance of the emphasis on distinctions and differences involved in informal reasoning. Historical explanations do not satisfy the convention which requires all true explanations to cite general laws which explain events. However, they satisfy the requirement of consistency, and they do cite a rule, i.e. a situation whose similarity can be used to explain the particular historical event in question. Lucas states: 'Similar situations often arise: what is meant by the claim that no two situations are exactly alike is that analogies must never be treated according to the scheme of [formal reasoning], with its rigid formulation of some rule or other which must always hold good, but according to the flexible method of [informal reasoning], where there is no demand that criteria be antecedently laid down and no knockdown falsification by counter-example. Parallels in history can often be drawn but must never be pressed.'[18]

The condition of consistency provides a key for understanding the assessment of judgements which, as Mitchell's argument demonstrates, is essential to informal reasoning. A judgement is guided by the condition of consistency and, therefore, must take into account the similarities and dissimilarities which are brought out in discussion. An individual's judgement about a particular argument involves assessing the relevant distinctions and differences from similar contexts. For example, a historian must take into account explanations of similar historical events in coming to a conclusion about the correct explanation of a particular event. His judgement will involve selecting the relevant features of similarity and using those to explain the event under consideration. Thus, his judgement is according to 'some' rule, though not one which is specified beforehand. But his judgement can be assessed by

[17] 'Lesbian Rule', p. 209.   [18] Ibid.

analysing the reasons which lead to his particular conclusion. For example, one can point out relevant distinctions and differences which the original judgement does not take into account. In this way the process of assessment proceeds.

It is important to note that dialogue between individuals is important for the advancement of an argument. The point to keep in mind is that the more scrutiny an informal assessment undergoes, the more evidence in the way of relevant differences and distinctions will be apparent. Singular reasons and judgements based on them require such criticism in a way in which formal reasons do not.[19] There is no other way to assess adequately particular conclusions than by the logic which is engendered by the formal requirement of consistency.

IV

A cumulative-case argument is related to informal reasoning as a deductive argument is related to deductive logic. In a deductive argument the conclusion is authorized by the deductive validity of the inference from the premisses. In a cumulative case, as Wisdom describes it, the relevant facts of the case 'severally cooperate in support of a conclusion'. Informal reasoning provides a way of understanding this notion of cooperating in support of a conclusion. In a cumulative-case argument the evidence takes the form of a set of singular reasons. Because of this, there is no general convention, such as the canons of deductive inference in deductive argumentation, which legitimizes inferring to the conclusion from the evidence. It is the lack of a convention about correct inferences in informal reasoning which distinguishes a cumulative case from an argument which involves a 'chain of demonstrative reasoning'.

If, as Mitchell claims, theism is justified on the basis of such a cumulative case, then the informal nature of the argument implies several things. First, it means that no specific inference rules govern the inference to the existence of God. This admission rejects from the beginning the proofs for God's existence in their traditional form and, by implication, the metaphysical

---

[19] Ibid. 208. The requirement of formal reasoning is consistency and constancy in contrast to consistency alone.

assumptions behind them. Secondly, it means that the reasons will be singular reasons. Hence, judgement will be required to assess the inference. Finally, it means that a particular type of argument will be appropriate to the assessment of theism. To argue against theism it will not be enough to challenge the inference with decisive counter-examples. The object of debate will be to counter the original assessment by showing how the reasons are inconsistently used. That is to say, the opponent will need to point to relevant differences and distinctions which indicate that these particular reasons should be assessed otherwise than supposed and on that basis lead to a contrary conclusion.

If we contrast a formal argument for the existence of God with an informal one, these implications will be clearer. Imagine a dialogue on the cosmological argument between Hume and Butler (hereafter referred to as H. and B.). B. begins the discussion with the assertion that God exists. The following dialogue illustrates the formalist approach:

B. God exists.
H. Why do you believe that?
B. It follows from the principle of sufficient reason that the world needs an explanation.
H. But there is no conceptual difficulty in saying that the existence of the world is uncaused. Therefore, there is no *necessity* by which we must say the world is caused, and your argument is unsound.

In this argument, which is actually very similar to the sort of response one finds in much contemporary literature,[20] B. tries to demonstrate the existence of God. For that reason he uses the formal conventions of deductive argument, and, therefore, the burden of proof is on him. He identifies two premisses, the principle of sufficient reason and a premiss about the existence of the universe, from which he infers the existence of God. H., in response, denies that B. satisfies the relevant conventions. He denies that the existence of the universe falls under the principle (that is, the unrestricted principle is false). B. is forced to defend the principle by showing that it does in fact apply with-

---

[20] This sort of objection seems rooted ultimately in Hume. But contemporary discussions seem to take this kind of counter-objection as decisive as well. See Mackie's analysis of the cosmological and teleological arguments in *The Miracle of Theism* for but one example.

out restrictions. So the burden of proof is on him. As Lucas says, 'the possibility of proof is a liability to prove; the initiative is rather a logical obligation than a logical privilege'.[21] If he is unable to accomplish that, his argument loses all logical force, and H. is left completely without reason to believe.

Contrast the formalist argument with the following account of the informalist approach:

B. God exists.
H. Why do you believe that?
B. Because the existence of God best explains the world. [Judgement]
H. But not everything needs an explanation. [Relevant distinction]
B. But I am not claiming that it does; rather I am guided by a much weaker principle that explanation is to be sought whenever possible. And my claim is that the world can be explained. [Denial]
H. But obviously you must admit that we have to stop the regress of explanation somewhere; so why must we go beyond the world itself. [Relevant distinction]
B. I do not claim that we have to go beyond the world; I say only that it is the best such explanation. There are other hypotheses about what is ultimate in the universe. [Denial]
H. But does that 'explain' anything; does not God have to be explained as well? [Relevant distinction]
B. Surely, by definition, God cannot be explained. But even so, the existence of God does explain. [Denial]

In this latter dialogue the burden is on H. to identify a relevant difference which would make B.'s initial judgement improper. Therefore, in the initial exchange H. tries to distinguish the world from those sorts of things which need explanation. And in the second exchange he distinguishes the world from those things which we have to take the explanatory regress beyond, or in other words, from those things which cannot serve as the end of the explanatory regress. In the third exchange he queries the assertion B. makes that God is a different sort of being from the world. This dialogue could continue indefinitely, but, throughout the exchanges, the challenges conform to the requirement of consistency rather than to a requirement which stipulates particular rules under which the argument must be subsumed.

----

[21] 'Lesbian Rule', p. 204.

This dialogue also illustrates the judgement which is necessary for the informal assessment of an argument. The initial
proposition is a judgement on the explanatory value of the
theistic hypothesis. So the claim is not that there is a formal
rule by which explanations such as theism can or should be
assessed, but that the existence of the universe provides a singular reason which is by implication open to assessment by
informal means. It is evident, to be sure, that there can be
arguments for the existence of God based on formal models, but
the argument as Mitchell takes it to be should be assessed as an
informal one. For that reason particular judgements are
criticized in a manner through which a reasonable judgement
about the evidential value can be made. An argument is
justified on the basis of the evidence brought forth in its
support, but, given the informal character of the argument and
the centrality of judgement, the process of assessing the evidence takes the form of drawing out relevant distinctions rather
than the subsumption of the premises under specified rules of
inference. In this sense the notion of a cumulative case refers to
the logical process involved in evaluating informal arguments.
In the dialogue a series of distinctions, differences, objections,
and counter-objections builds up. The final judgement is
cumulative, not only in the sense that the explanation is called
upon to account for a variety of data, but in the sense that there
must be a judgement on the cumulative weight of the various
objections and counter-objections.

V

One additional issue remains to be addressed: what is the connection between informal reasoning and the Bayesian methodology discussed in the two previous chapters?

The Bayesian methodology includes at least three different
features which need to be distinguished. First, Bayes's
theorem, as Swinburne uses it, represents the values of a set of
logically necessary relationships between propositions. These
relationships are termed 'epistemic probabilities'. Several
well-known interpretations of probability exist,[22] and Swinburne defends one of them, the logical theory of probability.

---

[22] Swinburne, *Confirmation Theory*, pp. 14–30.

The logical theory holds, among other things, that (1) there are propositions which state the probability relation between evidence and hypothesis, i.e. that there are propositions of epistemic probability, and (2) the probabilities stated by these propositions are independent of empirical matters. Swinburne notes: 'given that we understand by the evidence all our knowledge relevant to assessing whether or not the hypothesis is true, the probability of the hypothesis on the evidence is independent of further empirical considerations. The truth or falsity of a proposition of epistemic probability is then a matter of non-empirical considerations alone. It is a matter of what are our criteria for assessing evidence.'[23]

The second aspect of the Bayesian methodology is the claim that Bayes's theorem represents these probabilities. Given that there are these objective epistemic probability values, it is further claimed that they are related to one another in the way expressed by Bayes's theorem. Bayes's theorem is a deductive consequence of the axioms of the probability calculus; as such it is itself a logically necessary proposition which states logically necessary relations between the propositions of epistemic probability.[24] The Bayesian methodology accepts that Bayes's theorem represents the logically necessary relations between evidence and hypothesis.

The third aspect of the Bayesian methodology is the use of Bayes's theorem in assessing a particular hypothesis. In the case at hand, for example, Swinburne uses the theorem to clarify and support his claim about the weight of the evidence for the theistic hypothesis.[25] For this purpose he makes a number of methodological commitments. The first is to simplicity. He uses it to assess the various prior probabilities of the theorem. The second methodological commitment is to his particular understanding of explanation. Explanation is defined as either full or partial explanation, depending on the completeness of the entailment. If a hypothesis fully entails the evidence, it is a full explanation; if not, it is a partial explanation. The point is that he understands explanation in a way

---

[23] Ibid. 25–6. Swinburne discusses further theses on the logical theory; see pp. 24–8.

[24] Cf. ch. 3 on the probability calculus in Swinburne, *Confirmation Theory*.

[25] e.g. in *The Existence of God* on the cosmological argument, pp. 129–32, and on the teleological argument, pp. 144–8.

which allows for evaluating the predictive power of a hypothesis in terms of deductive entailment.

If separating these three features of the Bayesian methodology is plausible, we see what distinguishes it from the informal approach. As far as concerns the first aspect—the logical theory interpretation of epistemic probability—there is no conflict with the informal approach. Informalism does not entail any particular interpretation of the propositions of epistemic probability. In fact, in so far as reasons justify a conclusion, there is a sense in which they entail an obligation to accept the conclusion. This sense of universalizability attaches to any rational justification of an assertion, be it an informal or a formal justification.[26] Inasmuch as the logical theory, as opposed to some other theory of probability, best accords with this sense of universalizability, the informalist approach does not contradict it but rather supports it. The informal approach uses words such as 'probable', 'more likely', 'supports', and so on, in the same sense of justification and evidential support as any other approach to reasoning.

The second aspect of the Bayesian methodology is more difficult to judge. A huge body of literature on confirmation theory and the place of Bayes's theorem within it exists.[27] It must suffice to say that, though there are many objections to Bayes's theorem, it is not evident that the objections cannot be overcome. But even so, the informal approach advocated here does not deny that Bayes's theorem *per se* accurately represents the relations between propositions of epistemic probability. If there is any conflict between informalism and the Bayesian methodology, it will not be in any obvious way over the issue of whether Bayes's theorem in itself is acceptable.

If there is any conflict, it arises over issues associated with the third aspect of the Bayesian methodology. The crucial problem is that Swinburne uses Bayes's theorem as a tool for a formal argument for God's existence. Thus, throughout *The Existence of God* he assumes that specific conventions govern the evaluation of inductive arguments. Bayes's theorem represents the

[26] Cf. Lucas on the universalizability of informal arguments in *The Freedom of the Will*, pp. 38–9.

[27] Besides Swinburne, *Confirmation Theory*, see L. Jonathan Cohen, *The Implications of Induction* (London, 1970), Mary Hesse, *The Structure of Scientific Inference* (Cambridge, 1974), and Paul Howich, *Probability and Evidence* (Cambridge, 1982).

logic of confirmation, and only specific criteria are allowed as relevant for determining the probabilities. The prior probabilities of both the theistic hypothesis and the evidence are determined by applying the criterion of simplicity. And, by defining predictive power in terms of deductive entailment, entailment becomes the rule by which all full explanations are to be evaluated, both scientific and personal.

Swinburne provides a more developed account of reasoning in *Faith and Reason*. He holds that a person's inductive standards are 'his beliefs (whether explicit or not) about what makes what probable'.[28] These standards can vary from person to person, though some standards, for example, the principle of generalization, everyone must have. Further, we can determine a person's standards by watching him make inductive judgements. Swinburne describes the process of learning what a person's inductive standards are as follows:

Our claims about what are a man's inductive standards must be such that we attribute to him standards which license most of the inferences which he actually makes. We study the evolution of his beliefs. We see that when his evidence is e_1 he comes to believe h_1, and when his evidence is e_2 he comes to believe h_2, and so on. Our account of his inductive standards must be such as to make most of these steps legitimate; must be such that in general by them e_1 makes h_1 probable, e_2 makes h_2 probable and so on. . . . So given a set of information about which hypotheses a man judges probable on the basis of what evidence, we may set up a theory about his inductive standards which legitimizes most of his inferences.[29]

On this account, beliefs can fail to be rational in a number of ways. Someone's beliefs can fail to be properly justified by his own standards; if, for example, he forgets a relevant principle or has a false standard. The beliefs can fail to be rational also if they come about as the result of insufficient evidence or inadequate standards, either problem of which could have been corrected by proper research for more evidence or for better standards.

This description illustrates the extent of Swinburne's formalism for it shows that he does not allow for the possibility of singular reasons. Given that an individual's inductive

[28] *Faith and Reason* (Oxford, 1981), 43.   [29] Ibid. 43–4.

standards are known, we are then in a position to query the
legitimacy of his inferences since they will be based either
correctly or incorrectly on those standards. In this account of
rational belief, there are no cases where a person's judgements
are based on singular reasons, i.e. where his judgements cannot
be subsumed under a specific rule, either his own inductive
standards or ones which are known to be correct. In each case a
judgement about the person's rationality follows from an
application of previously determined inductive standards.
Rationality simply is the proper application of particular inductive standards.

The arguments of the earlier sections of this chapter give
reason to reject the formalist approach. But three further objections can be made to Swinburne's position. The first is a strictly
ad hominem argument. Though he correctly describes how one
might come to knowledge of someone's inductive standards, his
description of this process is surely artificial. The problem here
is that in ordinary reflection one never takes the time to
examine in detail someone's history in order to determine the
person's inductive standards. When one reads an article in a
journal, for example, one does not explore the personal history
of the author in order to find out whether he is using his inductive standards correctly. There is, to be sure, a distinction to be
made between judging a person's inference with reference to
his own standards and judging it with reference to the correct
standards. Typically, however, judgements about a person's
argument are not based upon a detailed examination of the
individual's past judgements. It is just not what is done in
assessing a person's arguments.[30]

A second objection rests on how we are to go about
determining a person's standards. When we construct a history
of someone's judgements in order to catalogue his inductive
standards, in so far as a generalization can be made at all, there
will be examples of inductive standards which do not fit the
generalization. For various reasons, some of which Swinburne
allows, there will be no perfect correlation between the set of
standards and the inferences the person makes. Any judgement

---

[30] We are not in a situation of radical interpretation, which is the proper venue, it
seems, for the sort of considerations Swinburne mentions. See Donald Davidson,
'Radical Interpretation', *Dialectica*, 27 (1973), 314–28.

about the person's standards will not capture all of the particular individual's actual use of his standards. Thus, when assessing his future judgements, one is never, in principle, in a position to know if the generalizations about his past standards apply to these particular judgements. From this it follows that one can determine only whether the person is following the same inductive standards he has previously followed, and not whether he is being irrational, for one is not in a position to know whether the standards he is using now are a misapplication of the generalized standards or whether he is using new standards. If the rationality of a person's beliefs is to be determined, there must be some way to assess the correctness of his inferences which is not the application of the inductive standards derived from past performance.

A third objection follows from Swinburne's account of how one comes to know which standards are correct:

Arguments can be used to show that certain inductive standards are the true ones (the true inductive standards being those which license all and only correct inductive judgements). Clearly the starting point of such investigation is a large set of judgements which seem to the investigator to be indisputably correct; that e_1 makes h_1 probable, but does not make h_2 probable; that e_2 makes h_2 probable, and more probable than h_1; and so on and so forth. As with all investigation we start from what seems to stare us in the face, although allowing for the possibility of later correction. We then seek, using the principle of simplicity, for the most natural extrapolation from those judgements, an extrapolation which would allow that we had made occasional mistakes but no more. Having reached an account of the true principles of induction we then see whether any necessary corrections to our initial particular judgements are ones which seem plausible. In so far as the general account which we reach fails to license judgements which seem, intuitively, to be obviously correct, we must look for another and perhaps more complicated account of the true principles of induction. But it may be that having formulated general principles, these seem so obviously correct to us that we change some particular judgements in the light of them.[31]

This description of how one comes to know which standards are the correct ones expresses very well Mitchell's argument concerning the necessity of judgement. In so far as some

---

[31] *Faith and Reason*, p. 47.

recalcitrant examples of inductive inferences do not fit well with the balance of other inferences, there are three options: '(a) the cases can be made to fit without distortion; (b) the cases are not genuine examples of reasoning; (c) the rules [i.e. inductive standards] have not been correctly specified'.[32] To decide between these options some judgement must be made, otherwise a vicious infinite regress ensues: 'To decide between these possibilities requires thought. If this exercise of thought has itself to be rule-governed, the question can in turn be raised whether these rules have been correctly specified, and so on *ad infinitum*.'[33] Therefore, in order to have a coherent account of how beliefs about the correct inductive standards are justified, even Swinburne's own account requires something similar to the sort of judgement indicative of informal reasoning. But if this observation is true, his formalistic account of rational belief cannot be correct. There must be reasoned conclusions which are probable, even in the strict sense of the logical theory, but which are not based on the application of general inductive standards.

We see then that there are points of contact between informal reasoning as presented in this chapter and Swinburne's Bayesian methodology. There is no conflict in the interpretation of probability nor about the assumption that Bayes's theorem in some way details the logical relations between the propositions of epistemic probabilities. But inasmuch as the Bayesian methodology is formalistic, there is a deep and ineluctable division between the two approaches. Given that formalism is incomplete without informalism, as reflection upon Mitchell's argument shows, there is little reason to believe that informalism reduces ultimately to the Bayesian methodology.[34]

It is appropriate to conclude this section with a comment on

---

[32] Mitchell, *The Justification of Religious Belief*, p. 89.   [33] Ibid.

[34] Swinburne's formalism is at the heart of the problem he has, as I see it, in coming to any definite conclusion on the probability of theism as an explanatory hypothesis. Gary Gutting notes that Swinburne's argument supports the contention that theism is a poor hypothesis at best. The difficulty is in applying such a criterion as simplicity with sufficient definiteness to generate a substantial probability. He spends 9/10 of his book assessing theism as an explanatory hypothesis on the basis of Bayes's theorem, and then gives considerable weight to an argument from religious experience based upon a 'principle of credulity' which is entirely independent of Bayes's theorem. See Gary Gutting, *Religious Belief and Religious Skepticism* (Notre Dame, Ind., 1982), 137–9.

the importance of the distinction between informal and formal reasoning. If belief in the existence of God is to be defended, some method for evaluating the evidence must be available. The burden of the first two chapters of this essay was to show that the Bayesian methodology cannot serve this function. Bayes's theorem cannot account for evidence as crucial as the existence of evil; nor can it easily accommodate radical conflicts over evaluative criteria. In this chapter I have sought to identify an alternative methodology for evaluating the evidence for the existence of God. The cumulative-case approach, and the notion of informal reasoning on which it is based, offers an alternative to the formal approach to justification. Because the cumulative-case approach allows for the inclusion of singular reasons, it can accommodate in the judgement about the evidential support for theism both the evidence of evil and the extensive variety of criteria. Judgements may vary about the significance of particular features of a cumulative case for the existence of God, but the approach itself provides a procedure for mediating between the conflicting judgements. For these reasons it is superior to the formal Bayesian methodology utilized by Swinburne.

INFORMAL REASONING AND RELIGIOUS BELIEF (2)

I HAVE argued that the logic of informal reasoning is the best way to interpret Mitchell's notion of cumulative-case reasoning. However, there are various ways to interpret Mitchell, and a number of different criticisms have been directed at his account of the rationality of religious belief. In this chapter I shall examine some of these criticisms in order to see whether they tell against the account of cumulative reasoning that I have constructed.

I

One objection almost everyone will have initially. Some may feel that the appeal to the informality of the argument is simply a diversion from the real issue, which is that there is very little evidence for theism and what there is is very weak. In cases where an argument is not sufficient to convince, the appeal to informality covers over the weakness of the case. Informal reasoning appears to be a crutch which allows one to believe on insufficient evidence.

Now it must be admitted that there is a certain 'softness' which comes with informal argumentation. The hard-nosed compellingness associated with deductive proofs or scientific experimentation is not evident. Still, it would be wrong to conclude from this softness that, in any relevant sense, informal reasoning is a lesser substitute for detailed critical assessment of evidence. In the first place, there are many examples of beliefs which are very strongly justified on the basis of informal reasoning. For example, historical beliefs such as the belief that Napoleon was defeated at Waterloo are surely as fully justified as inference can permit. No reasonable man could seriously challenge it even though it cannot be justified by formal means.

Informal arguments can be conclusive in this sense in those cases where the weight of the evidence is so great that no one could reasonably doubt the conclusion.[1]

It is wrong to distinguish between arguments based on the certainty of an argument's conclusion. Thomas Reid states this point nicely. He distinguishes between demonstrative and probable arguments by the kind of reasoning used in each.[2] He takes a probable argument, broadly speaking, to be any argument which is not based on demonstrative inference in the sense of deductively entailing the conclusion. Demonstration for Reid, however, does not lead to conclusions which are more certain than probabilistic reasoning. Rather, demonstration signals a different sort of reasoning altogether. Probable reasoning can lead to conclusions as conclusively justified as deductive ones. He states: 'The strength of probable reasoning, for the most part, depends not upon any one argument, but upon many, which unite their force, and lead to the same conclusion. Any one of them by itself would be insufficient to convince; but the whole taken together may have a force that is irresistible, so that to desire more evidence would be absurd. Would any man seek new arguments to prove that there were such persons as King Charles I or Oliver Cromwell?'[3] Reid intends by the concept of probable reasoning something similar to informal reasoning and insists that it can in principle lead to conclusions which are evidentially certain (even if they are not deductively entailed by surer premises).

These illustrations demonstrate that we can distinguish an informal argument from those which are simply weak ones. This is an important consideration. People are troubled by the diversity of belief and by the fact that religious disputes are not amenable to quick resolution. The existence of such

[1] Cf. J. R. Lucas, 'The Philosophy of the Reasonable Man', *Philosophical Quarterly*, 13 (1963), 97–106.

[2] 'In common language, probable evidence is considered as an inferior degree of evidence, and is opposed to certainty: so that what is certain is more than probable, and what is only probable is not certain. Philosophers consider probable evidence, not as a degree, but as a species of evidence, which is opposed, not to certainty, but to another species of evidence, called demonstration' (*The Works of Thomas Reid, D.D.*, ed. William Hamilton (Edinburgh, 1863), 482). Cf. also John Henry Newman, *An Essay in Aid of a Grammar of Assent* (London, 1901). See M. Jamie Ferreira, *Doubt and Religious Commitment* (Oxford, 1980).

[3] *The Works of Thomas Reid*, p. 482.

controversies confirms in the eyes of many that religious belief is irrational and leads others to doubt whether their own religious convictions are rationally acceptable. For this latter group, the appeal to informal reasoning could be a way out of their intellectual difficulties. And so it would be if the case for theism turned out to be strong enough. But it is important not to confuse the way in which one argues with the argument itself. No appeal to the type of argument employed can show that one is justified in holding a position: being justified in holding a belief is a matter of the weight of the evidence. The fact that one argues informally lends no weight positively or negatively to the conclusion.

But it is equally important not to underestimate the importance of informal reasoning. We can express this by drawing upon Roderick Chisholm's distinction between two radically different traditions of epistemological inquiry in Western philosophy.[4] One tradition finds its roots in Descartes, Hume, and Kant. This tradition attempts to answer the sceptic's question 'How can I know anything at all?', or 'How is knowledge possible?' A second tradition in epistemology seeks a less ambitious goal than to answer the sceptic. It accepts that we do in fact know some things, and it seeks to uncover the methods and structures of justification which are used in the pursuit of knowledge. Inasmuch as this tradition admits that some things are known, it rejects the severe scepticism of the first tradition. However, and this is the point of mentioning Chisholm's distinction, if we must rely solely on deduction or induction proper to justify our beliefs, we simply cannot get very far in uncovering the structure of justification for many kinds of belief.

Examples of this are similar to those mentioned earlier to illustrate informal reasoning. Hempelian deductive-nomological reasoning in science, for example, is generally accepted as the paradigm of rule-governed rational activity. But it fits poorly into a description of the structure of justification which admits only the inference patterns of induction proper or deduction. From general laws, it is claimed, predictions can be derived which lead to experimental confirmation

[4] Roderick Chisholm, *Theory of Knowledge* (Englewood Cliffs, NJ, 1966), 56–69. Cf. Roderick Chisholm, *The Problem of the Criterion* (Milwaukee, Wis., 1973), 12–15.

or disconfirmation of the general law. But the history of science shows that a scientific theory is rarely rejected on the basis of a single experiment.[5] Many experiments of different kinds must be conducted, and a judgement must be made about the cumulative evidential weight of the experimental evidence. In fact, the scientific community may acknowledge the presence of evidential anomalies, evidence which would be considered as decisive counter-examples under a more formal kind of argument, and accept the theory in spite of them. As with theories from many other disciplines, accepting a scientific theory or hypothesis involves informal reasoning.

Chisholm recognizes that an adequate epistemology must include reasoning which is neither inductive nor deductive. Referring to this as epistemic reasoning, he describes it as 'certain valid principles of evidence of the following sort: they are not themselves principles of inductive logic, but they are such that the application of them and the principles of inductive logic to e will yield the result that e tends to confirm h'.[6] On the surface Chisholm seems to give too much to the formalist, but he uses this concept of epistemic reasoning in conjunction with a capacity that he calls 'Verstehen', or 'intuitive understanding'. The problem of other minds, for example, leads to an acknowledgement of this capacity. He argues:

Perception, memory, and 'self-presentation' do not suffice to justify what it is that we know about the states of mind of other people, for no deductive or inductive argument based on the data of perception, memory, and 'self-presentation' will warrant any claim to such knowledge; hence, there must be additional epistemic principles. He will then formulate these principles by reference to Verstehen, or 'intuitive understanding'. The point would not be merely that in Verstehen, or intuitive understanding, we have a fruitful source of hypotheses about the mental states of other people; the point has to do with the justification of hypotheses. Thus, one may contend, for example, that the fact that a statement expresses one's Verstehen will confer some positive epistemic status upon that statement.[7]

[5] See Imre Lakatos, 'Falsification and the Methodology of Scientific Research Programmes', in Imre Lakatos and Alan Musgrave (eds.), Criticism and the Growth of Knowledge (Cambridge, 1970), 132–8.

[6] The Foundations of Knowing (Brighton, 1982), 87.   [7] Ibid. 92.

Intuitive understanding, a special case of Mitchell's capacity of judgement, is crucial to the very process of reasoning which is itself essential to the justification of what is known about other minds.

In the light of these examples, we can conclude that informal reasoning, though in its appearance soft, is not a case of trying to cover over weakness of evidence: as the examples show, there are some cases where informal reasoning leads to conclusive results, and, given a particular tradition of epistemology, informal inference is a needed complement to deductive and inductive inference in the description of the structure of justification.

II

Chisholm's description of Verstehen can easily be misunderstood. He does not clarify how it contributes to the justification of a proposition, or, as he puts it, how 'a statement expressing one's Verstehen will confer some positive epistemic status upon that statement'. Roderick Sykes recognizes a similar ambiguity in Mitchell's account of the status of judgement in cumulative reasoning and raises a number of related objections. His critique consists of two parts. The first queries the force of the infinite regresses which Mitchell uses to justify the place of judgement. The second questions the logical status of personal judgement.

Sykes identifies correctly the crux of Mitchell's argument for the necessity of judgement in reasoning. He writes:

There are two places, according to B. G. Mitchell, where . . . intuitive judgement is necessary to cut off an infinite regress of rules governing rules. In the first place, unless we use our judgement, we would have to use a rule that tells us when a rule of thought is properly applied, and then a rule to tell us when to use that rule, etc. In the second place, we may ask what it is that tells us what we should count as good reasoning. If not our intuitive judgement, it must be some further rule and what could justify that save either judgement or a further rule? And so on.[8]

---

[8] 'Soft Rationalism', p. 59. Sykes actually reverses the order in which Mitchell presents the argument, but this is immaterial to his argument.

Sykes believes that neither argument succeeds in establishing an independent role for judgement. He believes that Mitchell confuses different levels of judgement with an infinite regress. In the first argument, according to Sykes, Mitchell confuses a mistake about the proper use of a rule with a mistake in the use of a rule. Sykes believes that we can make mistakes in our second-order judgements about the proper rules without it in any way impugning our actual first-order use of the rules. Therefore, Mitchell's claim that we must make a decision about the proper use of rules in order to apply any rule properly is wrong. He concludes: 'Thus, the question of how best to describe our decision in applying a rule of thought is irrelevant to the question of how best to describe rational decision-making.'[9]

Mitchell's second mistake is to confuse a natural regress of justification with an infinite regress. As Sykes notes, since evaluative language is 'inherently justificational', the implicit openness to challenge always threatens to 'go off in an infinite regress'. The infinite regress that Mitchell identifies, Sykes believes, is endemic to the process of justification and not something peculiar to rule-governed reasoning: 'The problem with a regress of rules is the problem of a regress of justifications, and the latter problem arises whether one reads the notion of justification as an appeal to rules or as an appeal to intuitive judgement. So bringing in a judgement to stop a regress of rules only opens up the possibility of a regress of judgements.'[10]

Both Sykes's objections hang on distinguishing a non-vicious from a vicious infinite regress. He is right to distinguish the two, for there are many contexts where potentially infinite regresses are of no interest. For example, the potential infinite regress of explanations does not mean that a particular explanation is incomplete. The infinite regress is in that case benign.[11] Sykes's argument hinges on whether or not Mitchell has identified a *vicious* infinite regress. If the regresses are vicious, Mitchell's argument succeeds; if not, Sykes is correct.

A vicious infinite regress in the case of judgements would occur either if all the judgements must be made concurrently or, what amounts to the same thing, if, in order for the initial judgement to be made, the higher-level judgement must also be

[9] Ibid.   [10] Ibid. 60.   [11] Swinburne, *The Existence of God*, pp. 73–4.

made. And surely Mitchell's examples illustrate this kind of infinite regress. The point of his second argument is that, if the justification of a particular rule required the application of a further rule, the justification of the first rule would involve the justification of an infinite number of rules. In order to justify my use of a particular inference rule, I have to decide what examples exhibit the proper use of inference rules; but, in order to decide that, I must decide which rules should be used to decide which examples are relevant, and so on. And, in the first example as well, the point is that, in order to make the first judgement, a second must be made; and because the second judgement is similar to the first, a third must be made, and so on. Sykes believes that the infinite regresses are non-vicious. But, though he is correct in so far as he states that different levels of judgements are involved, he fails to come to grips with the true point of Mitchell's examples and fails to cast doubt on Mitchell's arguments.

It is clear that these arguments against the regresses do not work, but Sykes uses another argument which attacks the logical structure of informal reasoning. He comments: 'The difference must be noticed between a description of the psychology of an evaluative judgement ... and a description of its logical structure, which is to say of the justificational relations among the propositions that underpin it. Soft Rationalism [i.e. informal reasoning] must argue that intuitive judgement is adequate as such a *logical* description.'[12] (This brings out as well the ambiguity in Chisholm's description of the epistemic status of the faculty of Verstehen.) Here Sykes questions the role of judgement in justifying propositions, and whether the judgement itself adds anything to the evidence for the proposition.

Sykes begins his description of the logical value of judgement by identifying the character traits of the individual who judges a proposition worthy of acceptance. He cites Lucas's discussion of the 'stability of human character' in support of his contention that it is the particular quality of the character of an individual which lends epistemic weight to the judgement:

---

[12] Sykes, 'Soft Rationalism', pp. 60–1.

J. R. Lucas claims that 'on the whole our experience is that people who have been reasonable in the past will turn out to be reasonable in the future also'. . . . But how can we be sure that, in any instance of a particular reasonable man's judgements, his tendency to be reasonable is operative? Lucas' reply would be, I think, that we cannot be *sure*; but then we don't have to be, because a man's reasonableness is not just a single disposition. It is the result of a number of more or less independent character traits, and it would be very unlikely that these should all collapse in one instance of his judgement.[13]

Sykes takes Mitchell's position to be close to Lucas's and states of Mitchell: 'The ability to exercise rational judgement depends, he says, on having "appropriate intellectual, moral, and spiritual values".'[14] Sykes takes this as evidence that Mitchell covertly shifts the locus of rationality from, on the one hand, arguments conforming to rules to, on the other hand, arguers with particular character traits. Thus, in his view, informalism substitutes the reliance on people with good characters for the reliance on arguments with good logic.

Sykes attacks this shift as being a victory for 'obscurity'. He points out that it is no more secure to place the burden of rationality on the character of individuals than on the inference rules governing an argument. Therefore, though Mitchell appeals to judgement as if it is in some way epistemically valuable, it is not obvious to Sykes how such a judgement is supposed to protect rationality. He contends:

it is difficult to see how intuitive judgement can be sufficiently armoured against the possibility of error. If the virtues are not specifiable, the protection against error which they give is similarly non-specific. It is therefore useless protection. This is because if one doesn't know what one is ruling out as error then one hasn't guaranteed that unsuspected but possible errors aren't creeping in. Rules of thought, by contrast, have the advantage of clearly defining as in error anything that doesn't fall under their governance.[15]

This criticism is interesting. Sykes notes that personal judgement was brought in to complete, so to speak, our canons of rational assessment. Without judgement we are unable to assess rationally some kinds of proposition. But, as he points out, the virtues of a person's character are no more determinate

---

[13] Ibid. 61.   [14] Ibid.   [15] Ibid. 62.

than the rules they are intended to supplement. Therefore, the appeal to virtues secures rationality no more strongly than the appeal to rules.

At first glance this criticism seems full of insight. If the judgement itself contributes to a proposition's justification, it can be asked why it does so. If the judgement does not so contribute, no appeal to judgement will solve the problems generated by using rules. And if the contribution of the judgement is due to the character virtues of the individual, the same sort of regress arises which the original appeal to judgement was intended to overcome.

Sykes's mistake here is that he attempts to derive the importance of judgement in rational argument from personal character traits. He does not take into account the logical structure of informal reasoning. As he sees it, the use of judgement functions as an additional rule that somehow justifies the conclusion of an argument. He comments: 'Now [we] can respond to this argument of Mitchell's by asking of what exactly any of these virtues consists. *For to the extent that they could be exactly specified then they could be built into a rule.*'[16] But this interpretation of Mitchell misrepresents the entire intent of the appeal to judgement. Mitchell does not make judgement a 'rule'; rather, he demonstrates only that not all arguments can be of the sort which appeals to rules in order to justify a conclusion.

The point is that the sort of argument we are concerned with follows a different logic, a logic described earlier as guided by the requirement of consistency. The evaluation of evidence requires judgement, but the conclusion is not somehow made more secure than the evidence warrants simply for being the result of a personal judgement. One must judge what seems to be warranted by the weight of the evidence, and by definition in cases of singular reasons this is not justifiable by an appeal to some general rule.

However, the judgement about the evidence can be criticized by a challenge to the judgement's consistency. Further judgements will be needed in this process of criticizing the original judgement, but no infinite regress of judgements follows because the legitimacy of the original judgement is not dependent on making these further judgements. Thus, Sykes's

---

[16] 'Soft Rationalism', p. 62 (my italics).

original contention, that the infinite regresses in the application of rules were not vicious, actually applies in the case of informal reasoning. A first-order judgement does not require a second-order judgement for its justification.

Sykes was right to note the importance of personal virtues in the informalist account, but not in his assumption that they are meant to contribute to the evidential warrant for the conclusion. Indeed, these virtues are important, but they are so because we recognize that some people are better reasoners than others. Thus, an experienced scholar is likely to make better judgements than a first-year undergraduate. His training does not add to the logical value of his judgement; rather, the quality of his judgements reflects the training he has received.

Thus Sykes offers no substantial objections to Mitchell's argument, but he does help to clarify the argument because he represents an understandable error of interpretation of Mitchell, namely, to take the judgements necessary to informal reasoning as equivalent to further rules which in themselves justify a conclusion.[17]

III

Up to this point I have discussed objections relating to the concept of informal reasoning. There are also objections to using informal reasoning in the debate about religious belief. Chief among these is the claim that, though informal reasoning may be appropriate in scientific inquiry, it is not appropriate for the justification of religious beliefs. Thus, Gary Gutting has argued that the use of informal reasoning in science cannot be deployed to justify its application to the debate about theism.

He describes Mitchell's position as a 'Kuhnian justification of religious belief'.[18] Kuhn argues that scientific paradigms, or large-scale scientific theories, exhibit radical conceptual discontinuities.[19] Mitchell takes this description to apply to the

---

[17] Sykes brings forward a number of other objections. Though I believe they are important, they are not as forceful as the ones I have discussed here.

[18] *Religious Belief and Religious Skepticism*, p. 122.

[19] See Kuhn, *The Structure of Scientific Revolutions*, pp. 92–110. There is quite a debate on the nature of a Kuhnian paradigm. See also Margaret Masterman, 'The Nature of a Paradigm', in Lakatos and Musgrave (eds.), *Criticism and the Growth of Knowledge*, pp. 59–89.

differences between religious belief systems. He cites three points of comparison in support of his analogy. First, arguments between paradigms seem to be 'slightly at cross purposes'. The same phenomenon of being at cross purposes is evident in arguments between atheists and theists. Secondly, according to Kuhn, a paradigm-shift involves a large-scale reorientation of an individual's 'world'. A similar feature is obviously present in religious conversions. Finally, the language scientists use to describe a paradigm-shift is very similar to language used to describe religious conversions.[20] From these considerations Mitchell concludes that scientific paradigm-shifts and religious beliefs exhibit similar large-scale conceptual discontinuity between alternatives. However, over and against Kuhn, he goes on to argue that radical conceptual differences do not eliminate the possibility of rational choices between competing paradigms. Therefore, he argues, by analogy, since the shift between scientific paradigms is rational, selecting a religious world-view is as well.[21]

Gutting accepts that Mitchell has brought out some suggestive parallels between religious beliefs and scientific paradigms.[22] But ultimately, he believes, the comparison fails for two reasons. First, there is an important disanalogy which the comparison overlooks. The disanalogy follows from what he believes is one of Kuhn's most novel contributions. According to Gutting, Kuhn proposes a new interpretation of the authority of science. Of Kuhn he states: 'On his interpretation, the authority of science resides ultimately not in a rule-governed method of inquiry whereby scientific results are obtained but in the scientific community that obtains the results.'[23] The importance of the incommensurability of paradigms is that it highlights the authority of the scientific community. He comments further:

[20] Mitchell, *The Justification of Religious Belief*, pp. 69–70, cited in Gutting, *Religious Belief and Religious Skepticism*, p. 116.

[21] This a very attenuated account of both Kuhn and Mitchell; I seek only to fill out Gutting's description of Mitchell's suggestion as a Kuhnian approach to justification of religious belief.

[22] Gutting, *Religious Belief and Religious Skepticism*, p. 122. Gutting discusses Ian Barbour along with Mitchell as illustrations of the application of Kuhn's philosophy of science to the philosophy of religion. See Barbour, *Myths, Models and Paradigms*, pp. 8–11.

[23] *Religious Belief and Religious Skepticism*, p. 122.

But the incommensurability of rival paradigms means that the ulti-mate issue of debates about them will depend on the scientific com-munity's judgement as to the overall significance of the considera-tions urged by the various conflicting arguments. Given that scientists are specifically trained to make fair and informed judge-ments of this sort, Kuhn asks, 'What better criterion than the decision of the scientific group could there be?' This emphasis on the scientific community's judgement as the ultimate locus of the rational authority of science is a central feature of his account of science.[24]

According to Gutting, it is only because the scientific com-munity reaches a consensus on what theories are to be pursued that we have faith in the scientific endeavour. Without this basis in consensus there would be no authoritative discipline we call science. He writes: 'the mark of a scientific community is consensus about a paradigm. Without such consensus, there would be no unified judgement of the scientific community that could be put forward as authoritative.'[25] It is just this lack of consensus which makes the analogy to religious belief so prob-lematic: 'Because of this, the Kuhnian account of scientific cognitive authority cannot be extended to religion, where there are [sic] a wide variety of competing paradigms, without the consensus needed for a cognitively authoritative judgement. There is, of course, consensus within specific groups (in-dividual churches or sects). But taking the judgement of any one such group as authoritative is arbitrary, since there is no reason for preferring its judgement to that of numerous other groups.'[26] In his perspective Kuhn's account of the authority of science is coherent if, and only if, there is this consensus in the scientific community. Otherwise, there is no justification for accepting the judgement of trained scientists. Where consensus is absent, as in the case of religion, nothing warrants the judge-ments of individuals within particular groups. Therefore, Gutting concludes, choosing one group over another would be 'arbitrary'.

An obvious objection to Gutting is that he fails to make clear the particular role consensus plays in determining the rationality of science. His remarks about authority are espe-cially imprecise. Consensus may play a part in explaining why the results of science, in point of sociological fact, are so widely

[24] Ibid. 123.   [25] Ibid. 124.   [26] Ibid.

influential. In point of logic, however, the role of consensus is less obvious. Gutting appeals to consensus as a criterion for judging the rationality of a community: by the consensus in a community, we judge the rationality of its beliefs. Since there is very wide agreement within the scientific community, we trust the judgements of scientifically trained individuals. Unfortunately, in the case of religion, the consensus is absent. He concludes, therefore, that we cannot accept the beliefs of any single group within the community of religious believers.

However, interpreting the role of consensus in this way leads to counter-intuitive results. For example, it seems more natural to explain consensus by the common use of scientific methods and the weight of evidence than to explain the acceptability of a particular set of evidence and methods by the sheer consensus of the group. Further, consensus does not enter into the evidential considerations of the individual scientist. Scientists do not appeal to consensus as justification for their conclusion. If it is a criterion that does not guide the decisions of the scientists, it is a very strange criterion indeed. Surely the acceptability of the consensus is in some way a function of how well it accords with the evidence. It seems inconsistent to claim on the one hand that the judgements of trained scientists are good ones in the context of revolutionary science where there is, as yet, no consensus, but then, on the other hand, to say that those judgements are acceptable, not on the basis of their qualities of explanatory power, simplicity, and the like, but because they represent the consensus. Furthermore, if the authority of a scientific community is a function of the consensus within the community, it seems logically impossible to question rationally the consensus. But again this seems wrong. For history confirms that innovators have often been correct.

There are numerous other issues which Gutting raises. It is questionable, however, whether they address the thrust of Mitchell's suggestions. Surely the point of comparing scientific paradigms in periods of revolutionary science to religious world-views is precisely that there is no consensus in either community. The very lack of consensus makes the illustration pertinent for Mitchell's case. It is true that in science consensus develops, but this occurs when the shift of paradigm is complete. Even if Gutting contends that it is the resulting consensus which warrants the judgements of individual scientists during the period of revolution, this would cast no doubt on Mitchell's argument. For his point is that these decisions are rational ones, and they are not rule governed. If one looks simply at the logical form of the scientists' judgements during this period, they follow the informal model. And this is all Mitchell attempts to show by the parallel with paradigm-shifts.

Gutting's second objection also relates to the dissimilarity of the parallel. He argues that, if a religious world-view is a paradigm, it must in some way generate a problem-solving tradition. He says: 'A paradigm must also provide a basis for an on-going activity of problem-solving in the community that accepts it. Only a succession of successful problem solutions can provide the cumulative evidence that the community needs to form its judgement of the paradigm's continuing acceptability.'[27] The problem with religious world-views is that they do not generate any problems. They are compatible with practically everything.[28]

Gutting's assertion is correct: religious world-views do not generate the sort of problem-solving tradition which scientific paradigms do. At this point the analogy breaks down, as Mitchell admits. Obviously one difference between the two is the place of experimentation. Religion, as well as a number of other disciplines such as history or politics, is not experimental in the way that the hard sciences are. But it is simply untrue to say that there is therefore no evidence for or against theism which can warrant a continuing judgement of its acceptability. Gutting himself belies this conclusion when he follows up this argument with an examination of the various sorts of evidence claimed to support theism.[29] Inasmuch as it continues to be the best explanation for the range of data he supplies, there is a reason for its continuing acceptability. Gutting clearly identifies a difference between scientific paradigms and religious belief systems, but the difference would be important only if the capacity of the paradigm to generate problems were

---

[27] *Religious Belief and Religious Skepticism*, p. 125.

[28] Ibid. With the exception of the problem of evil, Gutting believes there is no problem-producing or problem-solving capability in theism. But even here he claims that theism offers little in the way of a solution.

[29] Ibid. 127–40.

essential to the exercise of the kind of rational judgement Mitchell believes is evident in paradigm-shifts. But, as Gutting states, the purpose of the problem-solving tradition is to generate evidence which allows the community to judge the paradigm's continuing acceptability. It would seem that as long as there is evidence to be explained, whether or not it is generated by the religious world-view itself, there is evidence on which the community can judge the viability of the religious world-view.

We have seen, then, that Gutting attacks Mitchell's use of Kuhn from two sides. First, there is an obvious lack of the sort of consensus in the religious community which is evident in the scientific community. His central claim is that the lack of consensus within religion casts doubt on our ability to judge rationally between religious belief systems. This conclusion is not obvious and in fact is counter-intuitive on several counts. The importance of consensus cannot call into question the logic of the judgements of trained scientists in periods of revolutionary science. In this respect the parallel between scientific paradigms and religious belief systems is evident. (It is a further question as to how much consensus is necessary for the judgements of a community to be authoritative, but it seems evident that any decision on that issue will illustrate yet again the sort of informal reasoning that Mitchell suggests is characteristic of arguments about religion.) Secondly, unlike scientific paradigms, religious belief systems fail to generate specific problem-solving traditions. For that reason, according to Gutting, they do not qualify as paradigms. However, as long as there is some set of data which continues to support religious belief, something that Gutting admits in a later section of his book, this disanalogy between science and religion is irrelevant. Gutting has shown—what Mitchell does not deny—that the analogy between religion and science does not hold in all respects. The question is whether it holds in the relevant respects. In the end, therefore, Gutting's objections to Mitchell offer no reason to reject the basic conclusion that religious world-views can be defended as the conclusion of an informal argument.

In this chapter a number of objections to the notion of informal reasoning have been perused. Much of the criticism directed at Mitchell's account is based on a faulty interpretation of it.

Given the interpretation that I have proposed, the various objections fail to succeed. It is clear, then, that the cumulative-case approach is an acceptable alternative to formal reasoning as the logic of arguments.

It was noted at the beginning of the discussion of informal reasoning that Mitchell's argument included two theses: one concerning the logic of the argument for theism and another concerning the nature of the theistic explanation. Since any argument for theism as an explanatory hypothesis, either formal or informal, will be only as good as its power to explain, we must now turn to an analysis of what it means to say that theism is an explanatory hypothesis.

5

THEISM AS AN EXPLANATORY HYPOTHESIS

SWINBURNE'S conception of explanation plays an important role in his interpretation and evaluation of the theistic hypothesis. Theistic explanation, on his account, is a personal explanation: God intentionally brings about various phenomena such as the existence of the universe (though, according to Swinburne, since we do not know what God's intentions were in acting to cause these phenomena, theistic explanation is at best partial explanation).[1]

This reading of explanation solely in terms of causality reveals a problem in his understanding of theistic explanation that parallels the problem with his use of Bayes's theorem. In Chapter 1 I argued that Bayes's theorem cannot fully account for all the evidence relevant for assessing theism. Theism explains certain evidence, for example, the existence of evil, non-causally. Thus, his concept of theistic explanation cannot be fully satisfactory. It fails to describe accurately theistic explanation just at that point where theism explains evidence in ways other than by identifying the cause of the evidence.

I have also argued that a particular interpretation of Mitchell's view of assessing cumulative-case arguments is superior to Swinburne's. My earlier conclusion has its parallel with the concept of theistic explanation. The concept of cumulative reasoning refers to the accumulation of many different types of evidence. This kind of argument Mitchell speaks of as an explanatory argument, one that 'makes better sense of' the data.[2]

Unfortunately Mitchell leaves uninterpreted this idea of 'makes better sense of', and he offers no explication of what sort of explanatory relation it is. Nevertheless, there is, I think,

---

[1] Swinburne, *The Existence of God*, p. 69.
[2] *The Justification of Religious Belief*, pp. 39–40.

implicit in his comment a notion of explanation that contrasts with Swinburne's concept of theistic explanation as the concept of informal reasoning contrasts with the Bayesian approach.

In this chapter I shall provide an account of theistic explanation that seems most appropriate as an interpretation of Mitchell's notion 'makes better sense of'. I make no claim that Mitchell in fact had this account of explanation in mind. The concept itself, however, is superior to Swinburne's in so far as it can accommodate various sorts of theistic explanatory power that Swinburne's account cannot.

I

The alternative to the strictly causal account of theistic explanation takes theism as an integrative explanation. In this description of the theistic hypothesis, the relevant sense of explanation is best described as integration, not causation.

Construing theism in this way is not novel. The concepts of world-views, paradigms, and metaphysical maps all suggest a similar idea of explanation in terms of integration rather than causation. As I noted in the Introduction, the sheer pluralism of concepts used to refer to this understanding of explanation contributes to the present-day confusion about theistic explanation.[3] However, the idea of integration itself needs some clarification.

In a broad sense, we have many analogues to the claim made for theistic explanation. Many scientific hypotheses, for example, are integrative explanations: they unite apparently disparate phenomena by postulating a single causal origin for them all. The theory about the atomic structure which led to the development of the table of elements is a case in point. By postulating the existence of a few atomic particles combining in regular ways, a single theory about the physical structure of a material object unified an enormous number of diverse physical phenomena.[4] Another example of a scientific theory's capacity for integration is the discovery of gravity. The theory about the

[3] See my Introduction.

[4] On the development of modern atomic theory, see René Toton (ed.), *Science in the Nineteenth Century*, trans. A. J. Pomerans (New York, 1965), 268 ff., and Edwin C. Kemble, *Physical Science: Its Substance and Development* (Cambridge, Mass., 1966), ch. 16.

gravitational field accounted for phenomena as diverse as the movements of the planets to the tides of the oceans. That is to say, the theory of gravity demonstrated the unity of a number of apparently independent phenomena by postulating a single causal mechanism common to each phenomenon.

These two examples illustrate how causality serves as an integrating concept. By postulating a single causal mechanism for many different, apparently diverse phenomena, the integrative capacity of both of these theories was high. And integration occurs not only with respect to causes, but also with respect to purposes and intentions. For example, postulating a single intention, say having the intention to play a soccer match, explains the purposes and intentions of actions as diverse as people exercising in order to get fit, others buying cloth to make kits for the team, and others gardening in order to prepare the pitch. That is to say, we can explain the many diverse purposes with reference to the one overarching intention to play the soccer match.

The idea of integration, therefore, refers to the capacity of a hypothesis or theory to demonstrate the unity of a number of apparently unconnected phenomena. To speak of integration as the central explanatory concept in a hypothesis is not to postulate an unusual explanatory concept. The basic idea, common to many types of explanation, is that the hypothesis unifies a diverse range of phenomena into a single coherent description. This definition is somewhat loose because it leaves unanswered the question concerning what it is about the explanation which serves as the integrating concept. I state it this way because, though an integrative hypothesis will use some concept as the central integrator, there is no single concept which serves that purpose in all explanations. Though integration can result from having a common causal mechanism, as is the case with the diverse chemical phenomena explained by atomic theory, causality is not the only possible integrating concept since, as we saw, purposes can serve a similar function.

One feature which distinguishes integrative explanations such as theism from integrative explanations such as the theory of gravity is their scope. Theism, or any similar hypothesis, is an explanation for the totality of experience.

The idea of an explanation of this kind is explicitly expressed by Ian Ramsey. Ramsey speaks of theism as an 'outline map'. By describing theism in this way he seeks to relate theism to metaphysics. 'Metaphysics', he asserts, 'arises from man's desire to know, in a world of change and transitoriness, just where he is journeying; it arises whenever man seeks to map the Universe and to plot his position within it.'[5] Ramsey's meaning is this: metaphysicians seek to give a measure of continuity to the apparent transitoriness of the universe evident in experience. For this purpose they postulate hypotheses about how the various features of the universe fit together. Metaphysical hypotheses make up for the lack of continuity by relating the particular features of the universe in such as way as to eliminate the apparent transitoriness. Though many different ways of relating the features of the universe are possible, theism, according to Ramsey, is one such map. It is a hypothetical map of the universe which uses the concept of God as the central integrating concept. He comments: 'The possibility of a metaphysical theology arises when . . . to unite the various metaphysical words that are cast up in this way, we use the word "God".'[6]

Stephen C. Pepper, though not speaking of theism, describes hypotheses of this scope as 'world hypotheses'.[7] According to Pepper, world hypotheses are demanded in order to resolve the conflicts and inconsistencies present in the corpus of human belief and knowledge (I shall use the term 'belief' to include both what we know and what we believe but do not know). Human belief encompasses many different kinds of subject areas, many different 'logical types'. What we believe ranges over such diverse fields as, for example, science, morals, politics, psychology, aesthetics, and religion. And, as Pepper recognizes, these beliefs are not isolated. Religious belief, for example, is not completely separate in content or in significance from our belief about right and wrong, nor is our understanding of politics completely isolated from either religion or ethics. To take a concrete example, an informed decision about the morality of abortion will rely on knowledge and opinion

---

[5] 'On the Possibility and Purpose of a Metaphysical Theology', p. 153. See also James Richmond, *Theology and Metaphysics* (London, 1970), 50–1.
[6] 'On the Possibility and Purpose of a Metaphysical Theology', p. 174.
[7] *World Hypotheses* (Los Angeles, Calif., 1942), 77.

about human biology and psychology, political theory, moral theory, anthropology, and possibly other subject areas as well. All these different topics have some bearing on a decision about the acceptability of abortion in a particular case. A second example is the question about whether a government ought to fund research and development of nuclear energy. In order to approach this question competently one must be conversant with political realities, economic necessities, the current state of scientific research on nuclear waste, moral theory, and so on.

Pepper's notion of world hypotheses relates to the coherence of human beliefs. One consequence of the great variety and diversity of beliefs is that they often conflict. Some scientific beliefs conflict with religious beliefs. There are some well-worn examples of this kind of conflict. Some religious traditions, by taking the Old Testament literally, teach that the universe was created in six 24-hour days and is in fact only a little over 6,000 years old.[8] These beliefs clearly conflict with the scientific results which suggests that the universe is well over 3 billion years old. Moreover, conflicts do not occur only between science and religion. Scientific knowledge sometimes conflicts with common sense also. Our initial impression, for example, is to believe that the objects of perception, say the computer on which I am presently typing, are solid objects. Some readings of science, however, assert that my computer is mostly space. Hence, there is a conflict, albeit a minor one, between the evidence of my senses and the dictates of science.

These examples serve to illustrate how conflicts can occur within the corpus of our beliefs. The evolution of a world hypothesis is a consequence of these conflicts. Though we may, and probably often do, hold inconsistent beliefs, if they are recognized as inconsistent, we are obligated to the best of our ability to excise that inconsistency from the body of our belief.[9] We do this by either adding other beliefs to or subtracting beliefs from the existent body of belief, but the process of making our beliefs systematically consistent and coherent requires creating hypotheses of the sort which we call metaphysical systems or world hypotheses. As we attempt to make

[8] According to Bishop Ussher, the genealogical tables in the Old Testament show that the earth was created in 4004 BC.

[9] Pepper, *World Hypotheses*, pp. 74–7.

our beliefs fit together, as we recognize the inconsistencies which are present, we are inevitably driven to a hypothesis which encompasses all of human belief within its scope. As long as some fact or belief lies outside the scope of the hypothesis, the possibility remains that it is inconsistent with some fact or piece of knowledge that lies within the scope of the hypothesis. We are, therefore, forced to broaden the scope of the hypothesis to include that isolated fact. A world hypothesis, therefore, is constructed in order to indicate how the totality of human belief is coherent and consistent. It is, as Pepper describes it, a hypothesis of 'unlimited scope'.[10]

An illustration of a world hypothesis is materialism.[11] Materialism unifies the phenomena of experience in a number of ways. In the first place, it asserts that everything that exists is fundamentally matter organized in various ways according to general natural laws. By making this claim about the ultimate nature of things, materialism takes as given the irreducible complexity of the organization of the universe into pieces of matter of finite size and various shapes. It explains the pluralism of experience by means of a single explanatory concept, namely, matter organized in regular, lawlike patterns. Though, on this view, there is no unifying causal origin for the universe (as theism asserts), there is a single substance of which everything consists. Materialism, therefore, represents a view about the physical constitution of the universe. However, as a world hypothesis, it also accounts for the phenomena of value and meaning in the universe. It does so by denying the existence of any objective, transcendental moral values and by affirming the ultimacy of human interest over any supposed divine interest. For example, Mackie, who is a materialist, in responding to the theistic claim that only God can give purpose to the universe, states: 'Still less do we need anything like a god to counter aimlessness. Men are themselves purposive beings. In their own nature they unavoidably pursue aims and goals; they do not need these to be given them from outside.'[12] By responding in this way to the theist, he, in his own way, answers

---

[10] Ibid. 72.

[11] The world hypothesis described by Pepper which comes closest to materialism is mechanism. See Pepper, *World Hypotheses*, pp. 186–231.

[12] *The Miracle of Theism*, pp. 249–50.

the very question which theism seeks to answer. Materialism, as a world hypothesis, is a comprehensive, integrative theory postulated to express the coherence of human belief about the universe.

II

Materialism is not a causal hypothesis, yet it serves to integrate by virtue of the way it interprets the universe in terms of the single kind of thing, namely, matter. This fact indicates why I distinguish causal explanation from integrative explanation. I distinguish strictly causal explanation from integrative explanations of unlimited scope because there are a number of different ways in which this integration comes about. Some are causal hypotheses and some are not. I have illustrated a non-causal integrative explanation with the example of materialism. Another example of a world hypothesis that does not integrate in terms of causality is the Hindu philosophy of Advaita Vedanta, which identifies the phenomenal world, the world of experience, with Brahman—ultimate spiritual reality.[13] The world of experience is not caused by Brahman, rather it is Brahman. Thus, Advaita Vedanta is similar to materialism in being monistic—interpreting reality in terms of one substance—but it differs from materialism because the ultimate reality Hinduism posits is not matter but spirit.

Theism, in contrast to both materialism and Vedanta, does include a causal element in its explanation. Indeed the most obvious questions theism answers are those concerning the causal origin of the universe. Certainly this is the motivation behind the traditional proofs for God's existence. Theism, however, explains a range of phenomena which goes beyond the range of things which need causal explanation; that is, theism explains not only the material world but also the meaning of existence, specific events in history, moral values, and other features of the universe. Because of its comprehensiveness, the sense of integration which theism achieves requires a much broader concept of explanation than that which Swinburne uses.

Part of the reason for construing theism as an integrative

[13] See Stuart C. Hackett, *Oriental Philosophy* (Madison, Wis., 1979), 123–66.

explanation is the inadequacy of treating theism as a strictly causal explanation. (I shall adopt Pepper's term 'world hypothesis' to refer to integrative hypotheses such as theism.) There are, however, several positive reasons for viewing theism in this fashion. The first concerns the ability of theism taken as a world hypothesis to account for the kinds of evidence that theism taken as a causal explanation cannot. In the next section of this chapter I discuss the evidence of evil with respect to theism as an integrative explanation, and in Chapters 6 and 7 I discuss other ways in which theism taken as a world hypothesis explains certain phenomena. Therefore, I shall reserve discussion of this particular reason until later.

The second reason appeals to the virtue of intellectual consistency. I have noted the vast diversity of beliefs and how particular beliefs are related to one another. Thus, an issue such as abortion reveals how ramified any informed decision is. But if these beliefs are related, they are also not, as a rule, totally consistent. Therefore, inasmuch as consistency is an intellectual obligation, a world hypothesis is unavoidable. Even someone like Mackie, who is suspicious of metaphysical schemes, must see the totality of his beliefs about the universe fitting into some sort of consistent system. Theism, in so far as it too provides a way to integrate the data of the universe, constitutes one possible world hypothesis.

The third reason stems from the obvious fact that people ask the kind of question that world hypotheses answer. These are questions of ultimacy. What is the meaning of life? What is the ultimate nature of existence? How does my experience fit into the overall scheme of things? The sense of wonder at the universe which surfaces so often as religious reverence is an expression of this same sense of questioning about the ultimate nature and purpose of existence.[14] People desire to know how things fit together, and for that reason they have questions which world hypotheses answer. Swinburne could claim that his intention is not to exclude theism as a possible answer for these sorts of questions. Indeed, it would seem definitionally true that God, as the creator and sustainer of the universe, would have purposes for creation that would give meaning to human existence. However, the problem with Swinburne's formulation of

[14] See Anthony O'Hear, *Experience, Explanation and Faith* (London, 1984), 143–85.

theistic explanation is that he ignores the power of theism to answer these questions when he assesses the explanatory power of theism. That is to say, even though Swinburne could admit that theism can answer these questions, he does not consider them important for assessing the evidential support for theism. By contrast, speaking of theism as an integrative explanation makes the ability of theism to answer questions of ultimacy a central feature of its overall explanatory power.[15]

Swinburne, in defining explanation in terms of causality, tries to provide a general account of explanation. However, any attempt like his is bound to fail because of the particularity of explanations. Explanations are given as answers to questions, but not all questions are concerned with causal origins. Explanations are given by scientists to other scientists, by theologians to other theologians, by teachers to pupils, by parents to children, and so on. What all these contexts have in common is that, in each case, an explanation is given in response to some question. The scientist answers questions about, for example, the physical make-up of a chemical compound; a mother answers a child's questions about the meaning of the fairy-tale; a historian answers a question about the historical significance of the Magna Carta. As J. R. Lucas comments, 'Explanations are answers. They are answers to questions, asked or anticipated, and in particular to the question "Why?".'[16]

Peter Achinstein suggests an account of explanation which seems to capture this contextualism. He relates explaining to understanding: 'When S explains q by uttering u he intends to render q understandable; he intends to enable others to understand q.'[17] Achinstein's idea is that when a person does not understand something, he asks for an explanation of it. The ensuing product of the explaining act, namely, the explanation, allows the person to understand what previously he did not.

I mention this view of explanation, though I have not argued for it, because it is sufficiently liberal to allow both Swinburne's conception of explanation and the sort of theistic explanation envisaged in this essay to be legitimate kinds of explanation.

---

[15] See ch. 7.   [16] *The Freedom of the Will*, p. 33.
[17] *The Nature of Explanation* (New York, 1983), 63. See also his earlier work, *Law and Explanation* (Oxford, 1971), ch. 4.

What constitutes a proper explanation is determined contextually by the question which is asked and by the person who asks it. Thus, by asking the teacher to explain the meaning of, for example, a particular Latin word, the language student is requesting some additional information about the word, maybe a synonym, which will make the word understandable to him. The scientist, requiring empirical tests to confirm his hypotheses, seeks to understand the underlying physical mechanisms of the universe. The individual who looks for a world-view such as theism or materialism that is capable of providing a consistent and systematic representation of the organization of the universe seeks to understand how the great diversity of the universe fits together. In each case what constitutes a correct explanation will depend on the question and the context in which it is asked.

One way to conceive of the difference between theism as an integrative explanation and theism as a strictly causal explanation, then, is by contrasting the kinds of question each attempts to answer. For Swinburne the existence of God answers a much narrower set of questions than those envisaged here. Explanations based on causality are not necessarily incorrect, but the conception of theistic explanation on which they are grounded is unnecessarily and inappropriately narrow. By defining theistic explanation in the way that he does, Swinburne puts constraints on the theistic hypothesis which hinders an adequate assessment of its true explanatory power.

III

Many people have objected to taking theism as an explanatory hypothesis because of disanalogies between theistic explanation and scientific explanation. Mackie, for example, criticizes theism because it does not differentially explain. He states:

however, [there] are general constraints which apply to explanatory scientific hypotheses and theories of whatever sort. . . . But is there some reason to suppose that these constraints are particularly damaging to the theistic hypothesis as an explanation of the 'marks of design'? I think there is, because the theistic hypothesis does not *differentially* explain specific phenomena in the way that successful scientific theories do: it does not explain why we have these phenomena rather than others. A scientific hypothesis is often confirmed by its success in explaining exactly what is observed, by tying up what on an alternative view remain as loose ends, and perhaps by predicting further, otherwise unexpected, observations which are then made, or possible constructions which are then successfully carried out. This the theistic hypothesis does not do.[18]

Mackie demands of theism that it account for the particularity of the phenomena. In one respect his objection is odd because, though he is specifically criticizing Swinburne, in fact, on Swinburne's account of theistic explanation, the existence of God gives a very specific reason why there is just this much order in the universe and not some other amount: God desired to create a world that is both good and such that humans have the opportunity in it to mature in knowledge and character, and the amount of order in this world is just right for God's purposes.

But even if we allow Swinburne's argument as adequate, Mackie's criticism makes a relevant point. The analogy between scientific and theistic explanation is weak. The problem, as he sees it, is that scientific explanations typically are much more empirically fruitful than theism in tying up loose ends and leading to predictions.

However, though his description of theism may be accurate, Mackie may also be demanding of theism that it satisfy a condition which he concedes that other explanations of its type do not have to satisfy. This can be illustrated with an example of Mackie's own construction. Other metaphysical hypotheses exhibit the same lack of differential explanation which he finds offensive with respect to theism, but, in these other cases, he endorses the hypothesis.

Consider the case of realism versus phenomenalism. Realism is the hypothesis that extra-mental objects exist independently of our perceiving them and that they cause our perception of them. In the discussion of the veil-of-perception problem in his *Problems from Locke*, Mackie answers the question whether objects exist independently of our perception of them, whether or not there is anything behind our perceptions. Mackie is a realist because he believes that the evidence confirms realism more than its alternatives.

[18] *The Miracle of Theism*, p. 138.

He refers to realism as an 'outline hypothesis'.[19] Further-more, part of the explanatory power of outline hypotheses such as realism is that they unify data. Mackie calls this a special sort of simplicity, 'the elimination of unexplained coincidence'. In the case of realism this means filling in gaps in our experi-ence. Mackie states it this way:

What is essential to this outline hypothesis is that it fills in gaps in things as they appear, so producing continuously existing things and gradual changes where the appearances are discontinuous. Its result-ing merit is a special sort of simplicity, the resolving of what would, on the rival, phenomenalist view, be quite unexplained coincidences: what we now regard as successive observations of the same thing at intervals would be the repeated springing into existence of complex groups of appearances remarkably like other groups which had passed out of existence before.[20]

Realism, on this view, brings together a number of apparently unconnected phenomena and unifies them by postulating the existence of extra-mental objects which cause the experiences we have. For this reason it is superior to phenomenalism.

Mackie criticizes theism because it is not a differential expla-nation, but the explanations envisaged here are not differential explanations either. Though he believes that realism is clearly superior to phenomenalism, it is not because the hypothesis differentially explains the phenomena. Indeed both realism and phenomenalism 'leave the world as it is'. They are not scientific hypotheses, but rather they are more general theories within which scientific theories are constructed.[21] The hypothesis of realism does not support any predictions about the future state of affairs, nor does it tell us why the world is like it is. Only after we assume the truth of realism is there any basis for differential explanation. Once realism has been given initial credence by its capacity to integrate the data, our experience of causal interaction and our research into the psychology of per-ception provide continuous corroborative evidence. Thus, the vicious circle of confirmation becomes, as Mackie describes it, a 'virtuous spiral'.[22]

The point at issue here is whether it is a deficiency of a

---

[19] J. L. Mackie, *Problems from Locke* (Oxford, 1976), 51–5.
[20] Ibid. 64.   [21] Ibid. 67.   [22] Ibid. 66.

hypothesis such as theism that it does not exhibit the sort of differential explanation characteristic of scientific hypotheses. It seems that it would not be a deficiency if the model for theistic explanation is not scientific explanation but is, as has been argued in this essay, explanation along the lines of Mackie's conception of realism. His example illustrates how a criterion such as simplicity can guide one's selection of a particular hypothesis even though the hypothesis does not differentially explain the evidence.

Many criteria may apply to a particular case. Mackie applies a single criterion, simplicity. Obviously simplicity is one criterion: the simplest hypothesis, other things being equal, is the most likely to be true. However, as we argued above, a number of different kinds of simplicity may be important to a particular evaluation. Here the importance of informal reasoning is evident, for it takes an informal judgement to apply and assess the various criteria of simplicity. This is evident in Mackie's example because, though realism simplifies by unifying the otherwise unconnected appearances, phenomenalism simplifies by having only one kind of thing, namely, appearances. Phenomenalism has an ontological simplicity that realism lacks. Mackie gives no consideration to the value of the simplicity of phenomenalism, but it is obvious that he judges a certain kind of simplicity, namely, the unifying of otherwise unconnected appearances, to be most relevant.

This same conflict among criteria is a characteristic of assessing world hypotheses. For example, if we evaluate two hypotheses, theism and materialism, on the basis of simplicity, we also find that, though they both simplify, they simplify in different ways. Theism simplifies by making everything depend upon the power and will of God. The decision of an infinite immaterial Spirit explains all contingent reality with its various characteristics. But theism implies a certain kind of dualism: spirit and matter. Materialism, in contrast to theism, eliminates this dualism by construing everything which exists as composed of matter governed by natural laws. Everything reduces to a single kind, namely, material objects. Materialism, therefore, exhibits the same kind of ontological simplicity as phenomenalism, a simplicity that theism does not have. So, in trying to evaluate theism and materialism, we see a

variety of relevant kinds of simplicity. However, as my argument shows, the importance of each kind of simplicity to a final
evaluation cannot be determined by the application of a formal
method. Rather, there must be a judgement about the relative
weights in the context of an assessment of the overall balance of
evidence. And this judgement must be an informal one.

I noted above that interpreting theism as a world hypothesis
rather than as a simple causal explanation has the further
advantage of illuminating the evidential connection between
evil and the theistic hypothesis in a way that Swinburne's
approach is unable to do. The connection involves the integrative function of theism. Consider again the dialogue between
the theist and the materialist. The theist will point out that the
ontological simplicity materialism achieves has a cost, namely,
that materialism must reduce the mental to the physical, a task
which is highly controversial philosophically.[23] The materialist, on the other hand, will point to the existence of evil as
evidence against the existence of an all-good and all-powerful
God, and the theist must admit that there is here a discrepancy;
there is something that he cannot fully explain. This lack of
completeness in the theist's case counts against his position.

These various objections arise because there is an apparent
failure in each world hypothesis to integrate the data of the
universe completely. Thus, the dialogue between them reveals
a second criterion that is important for evaluating world
hypotheses, comprehensiveness. Each of the protagonists in the
debate identifies areas which the alternative world hypothesis
does not appear to encompass completely. The theist does not
believe that materialism 'saves the phenomena' of personal
experience, while the materialist believes that the existence of
God does not cohere with the experience of evil.

We see, then, that a metaphysical world hypothesis must
satisfy many different criteria. We have looked at two: simplicity and comprehensiveness. The application of these criteria
illustrates informal judgement at work. Judgement is essential
for any assessment at all of a particular world hypothesis.

---

[23] I assume here that materialism entails the truth of some kind of mind–brain
identity theory and that theism entails the truth of some more substantial difference
between mind and body. Jerome Shaffer provides a good introduction to the problems
of both positions. See Jerome Shaffer, *Philosophy of Mind* (Englewood Cliffs, NJ, 1968),
ch. 3.

IV

If theism is a metaphysical world hypothesis, it is a mistake to speak of theism generically rather than of Christian theism or of Islamic theism or of some other kind of theism. Most ordinary religious believers, it seems, from whatever tradition of theism, grow into, or are converted into, a particular type of theism and not into some general theism which at a later point becomes transformed into a distinctive kind. To be sure, traditional philosophical arguments for the existence of God have had such a two-step character. St Thomas, for example, first proves the existence of an uncaused cause and only then defends Christian theism.[24] But this shows the difference between the more direct approach of the traditional arguments, based as they were on a major premiss such as the principle of existential causality, and the integrative approach taken here. The traditional two-step apologetic involved a quite different kind of argument from that envisaged in the present case. It involved a deductive proof. Once the deductive approach is abandoned, as I have assumed it should be, the philosophical motivation for such a natural theology disappears.

Hence, the logic of integration runs counter to defending a general theism rather than a particular version of theistic belief. World hypotheses are by definition proffered to explain as comprehensive a set of phenomena as possible, namely, everything in the world, and this global character of the hypothesis makes impossible a distinction between evidence which confirms a generic theism and evidence which confirms, for example, Christianity. Inasmuch as a generic theism accounts for the data of the universe, it competes with Christian theism.

Another reason for working with a more specific type of theism in the debate about the rationality of religious belief relates to the nature of the hypothesis itself. Theistic explanations of all varieties emphasize the ultimately personal nature

---

[24] The idea of a two-step apologetic has a parallel in the distinction between natural theology and revealed theology. Thomas, for example, believed that the existence of God could be proved by reflection on the natural world, but that the truth of dogmas such as the incarnation and the Trinity can only be known through revelation. This process of proving, first, the existence of God and, secondly, the truth of Christian theism is what I call the 'two-step apologetic'. Cf. book 1 with book 4 of Thomas, *Summa Contra Gentiles*, trans. Charles J. O'Neil (Notre Dame, Ind., 1975).

of the universe. Any theistic hypothesis integrates the phenomena of experience in part by describing the universe as an expression of God's purposes, and any specific version of theism
has some commitment concerning the nature of those overall
purposes of God. The response to the problem of evil illustrates
well the diversity among the theistic traditions concerning
God's purposes for creation. In Christian theism, for example,
God's desire to relate to creatures with the freedom to respond
in love is fundamental. But creating creatures with free will
according to Islamic theism is not a part of God's purposes for
the world, and, hence, it is not a part of theodicy.[25]

Even more fundamental differences with respect to God's
purposes exist if one considers the ideas which serve to define
each tradition uniquely. The Christian idea of God's purposes,
for example, revolves around the exemplary love exhibited in
the incarnation, atonement, and resurrection of Christ. In contrast, Hebrew theism emphasizes the revelation of God in the
election of Abraham and in the providential care of the nation
of Israel as illustrated by the Exodus. The point is that we
cannot reduce the specific divine purposes and intentions in the
theistic hypothesis to the lowest common denominator among
the variety of theistic systems. These are different explanatory
hypotheses. If the strength of a theistic explanation is tied
directly to God's purposes, the hypotheses will have very
different explanatory powers.

These observations lead us directly to Swinburne's objection
to including specifically Christian doctrines in the hypothesis
of theism. He refuses to incorporate into his explanation of evil
doctrines such as life after death and the redemptive incarnation because, in his view, doing so would unduly complicate
the theistic hypothesis. Given the importance of simplicity for
evaluating theism, the addition of these hypotheses reduces its
prior probability, and, therefore, more confirming evidence is
required in its support.[26] His argument has some force, for, if
simplicity is a criterion at all, a generic theism is obviously
simpler in some ways than Christian theism. But if the theistic
systems are taken as world hypotheses, Christian theism and

[25] Arthur Jeffery provides an interesting survey of predestination in Islam. See
Arthur Jeffery (ed.), *Islam: Mohammad and His Religion* (New York, 1958), 147–54.
[26] Swinburne, *The Existence of God*, pp. 221–2.

generic theism are competing alternatives. Hence, to this extent, Swinburne gives reason to accept generic theism and to reject Christianity, and, if Christian theism is to be preferred, it will have to be superior to Swinburne's generic theism in some other way.

This implication serves to highlight the distinction between Swinburne's description of theistic explanation and the description given in this essay. On the integrative view, there is no evidence which confirms Christian theism that is not also part of the evidence which the generic theism must explain; and, given that the purposes of God are essential to the explanatory power of either hypothesis, generic theism, with its minimal description of God's purposes, will have an explanatory power different from that of Christian theism. Swinburne rejects both of these features of the integrative account in his defence of theism. I have argued that his approach to theistic explanation is crucially inadequate in a number of ways. If this is correct, we have good reason to deny the force of his objection and to examine Christian theism as an alternative to his generic theism on the basis of its integrative power.

In this chapter I have argued that theism is best taken as an integrative explanation, a world hypothesis, rather than as a strictly causal explanation. The idea of theism as an integrative explanation, however, needs further development. I have claimed that a world hypothesis is postulated to explain the totality of human belief. Theism accomplishes this explanatory function in part by postulating the existence of a logically necessary person with specific intentions and purposes for the world. In the following chapters I shall examine this central feature of the theistic hypothesis.

6

CAUSALITY, MEANING, AND THE CONCEPT OF GOD

THEISM, as a world hypothesis, attempts to make sense of the universe. It remains now to be seen how theism accomplishes that task. In this chapter I shall examine some of the features of theism which facilitate this integrative function. The central concept of the theistic world hypothesis is that God is a person. By considering God to be a person, we bring together in theism two integrating ideas: causality and purposiveness.

I

The most obvious piece of evidence for the existence of God is the universe itself. Some, however, have argued that it is incoherent to ask for an explanation of the universe as a whole. Russell, for example, in his debate with Copleston suggests this very thing. Copleston claims that the world as a whole needs a cause, and Russell's reply typifies this response. He asserts that the very question of the cause of the universe is quite meaningless, and he offers an analogy to illustrate his claim: 'I can illustrate what seems to me your [i.e. Copleston's] fallacy. Every man who exists has a mother, and it seems to me your argument is that therefore the human race must have a mother, but obviously the human race hasn't a mother—that's a different logical sphere.'[1] In his view, to ask whether the universe as a whole has a cause is a category mistake.

A second analogy exemplifies a contrasting view on the matter. This analogy is credited by Samuel Clarke to the 'able writer' of *Religion of Nature Delineated*:

[1] Bertrand Russell and Frederick Copleston, 'The Debate', in John Hick (ed.), *The Existence of God* (London, 1964), 175.

Suppose a chain hung down out of heaven from an unknown height; and, though every link of it gravitated toward earth, and what it hung upon was not visible, yet it did not descend, but kept its situation. And, upon this, a question should arise, what supported or kept up this chain? Would it be a sufficient answer, to say, that the first or lowest link hung upon the second, or that next above it; the second or rather the first and second together, upon the third; and so on in infinitum? For what holds up the whole? A chain of ten links, would fall down; unless something, able to bear it hindered. One of twenty; if not staid by something of a yet greater strength, in proportion to the increase of weight. And therefore one of infinite links, certainly; if not sustained by something infinitely strong, and capable to bear up an infinite weight. And thus it is in a chain of causes and effects; tending or (as it were) gravitating, towards some end. The last, or lowest depends, or (as one may say) is suspended upon the cause above it. This again, if it be not the first cause, is suspended, as an effect, upon something above it, etc. And if they should be infinite; unless (agreeably to what has been said) there is some cause, upon which all hang or depend; they would be but an infinite effect, without an efficient. And to assert there is any such thing, would be as great an absurdity as to say, that a finite or little weight wants something to sustain it, but an infinite one (or the greatest) does not.[2]

Both Russell and Clarke appeal to the intuitive force of distinct pictures of the universe as a whole. Clarke suggests that the proper analogy is the chain hanging out of heaven, while Russell believes that the analogy to motherhood is closer to the truth. These beliefs represent contrasting a priori assumptions about the nature of the question being asked. Clarke is of the opinion that to refuse to ask the question is absurd, while Russell believes to ask the question is meaningless. Of course, to admit that the question is meaningful is not, as Clarke seemed to believe, to prove deductively the existence of God. As Swinburne rightly points out, from the standpoint of evidence, the universe could be a brute fact and for that reason inexplicable. However, there is no need to go as far as Russell and deny the very propriety of the question. Theism does offer one rational explanation for the existence of the universe which undeniably has some explanatory power, even if it is, in the judgement of some, small.

---

[2] 'A Demonstration of the Being and Attributes of God', in *The Works of Samuel Clarke*, ii (London, 1738), 526, n.d.

The explanatory power of theism with respect to the existence of the universe lies in the fact that theism postulates a single causal origin for the universe. Theism, as Swinburne argues, simplifies our picture of the universe because it reduces all causal explanation to personal explanation in terms of a single omnipotent, omniscient God. Against the protests of Russell, this much must be admitted. The notion of causation by a single person is part of the integrating power of theism. Every contingent thing that exists, it is claimed, exists ultimately by the power and will of God. Therefore, the universe with all its diversity can be seen to have a single origin in God.

Swinburne speaks of God as a person. God, in his view, is a 'person, without a body (i.e. a spirit) who is eternal, free, able to do anything, knows everything, is perfectly good, is the proper object of human worship and obedience, the creator and sustainer of the universe'.[3] The property of being a person, on this view, is essential to being God; or, stated obversely, something which does not have the property of being a person is not God.

Swinburne describes what it means to be a person using Peter Strawson's concepts of M-predicates and P-predicates.[4] The notion of P- and M-predicates refers to the sorts of features that are characteristic of things which we call 'persons'. P-predicates are those which describe persons in respect of having consciousness. For example, 'is smiling' and 'is writing this chapter' are examples of P-predicates because they connote conscious activity. Other animals exhibit conscious behaviour also, and so only certain P-predicates characterize persons. For example, 'speaking his mind' and 'making moral judgements' are predicates ascribable to persons, but not to animals. P-predicates can be distinguished from M-predicates. M-predicates ascribe properties that qualify a person as a material body. Thus, 'has brown hair' and 'weighs 100 kilograms' are M-predicates. P-predicates apply only to persons. A person, hence, is anything to which predicates of the right sort properly apply. Many of these kinds of predicates apply to God, mainly P-predicates, but some M-predicates also, and, therefore, God is a person.[5]

---

[3] *The Coherence of Theism* (Oxford, 1977), 1.
[4] Ibid. 100–2. Cf. P. F. Strawson, *Individuals* (London, 1959), 103–10.
[5] *The Coherence of Theism*, pp. 102–4.

Though many believe that this unqualified ascription to God of the property of being a person is unduly anthropomorphic, the description reflects the integrating feature of the concept of God as a cause. Part of the integrating power of theism lies in the fact that it postulates a single personal origin of the contingent universe. Since Swinburne, for example, introduces God as part of an explanatory hypothesis, he must postulate a concept of God commensurate with our understanding of causality and of theoretical terms. Otherwise his argument and the nature of the postulated God would be incompatible.

According to Swinburne, as we noted in the last chapter, personal explanations differ from scientific ones because the intentions of rational agents are not reducible to descriptions of natural laws. Conceptually, therefore, there are only two possible kinds of causal agent: rational agents and non-rational agents. (Typically we speak only of two specific kinds of agent: inanimate material objects and persons of some description. In what follows I shall use Strawson's typology, 'persons' and 'objects', to refer to the two kinds of agency, but I shall use the term 'objects' in a very liberal sense to include the possibility of causation by non-rational, non-material agents.) Therefore, if a phenomenon is to be explained causally, it must be explained either by an instance of the essential kind 'person' or by an instance of the essential kind 'object'.

We can see, therefore, how the concept of God gains content in the context of a philosophical justification for theism. The particular attributes of God result from maximizing attributes essential to being an instance of the kind 'person': all-knowing, all-powerful, and so on. The fact that the concept of a person can be used as an integrating concept does not mean that it is necessarily a good concept for this purpose. Other concepts can also be used. The essential kind 'object' has a similar kind of integrating power, and, therefore, a world hypothesis which postulates a single non-personal ground of existence would have a similar kind of integrative explanatory power. For example, Spinoza's concept of substance is one variety of a non-personal integrating concept.[6]

The fact that causal notions influence the formulation of the

[6] Benedictus de Spinoza, *Ethics*, trans. Andrew Boyle (London, 1959), 1–36. In pt. 1, Spinoza develops his view on substance.

concept of God is not peculiar to contemporary philosophy of religion. It is just as strongly evidenced in Scholastic arguments for God's existence. When one examines the Five Ways of St Thomas, the dependence of each argument on Aristotelian cosmology is obvious.[7] The First Way, for example, is an argument from change:

For to cause is to bring into being what was previously only able to be, and this can only be done by something that already is; thus fire, which is actually hot, causes wood, which is able to be hot, to become actually hot, and in this way causes change in the wood. Now the same thing cannot at the same time be both actually x and potentially x, though it can be actually x and potentially y: the actually hot cannot at the same time be potentially hot, though it can be potentially cold.[8]

The argument continues until it reaches a being which is the first cause of change, not itself changed by anything. And this, he notes, is what everyone understands by God.

For Thomas the description of God as 'that which cannot change' has a very determinate meaning. Change involves actualizing the potential within a substance. God is pure act and has no potential. Furthermore, these categories of actuality and potentiality provide the basis for the derivation of the concept of God. In questions 3–11 of the *Summa Theologica*, Thomas elucidates the attributes of God in terms of the notion of pure actuality. For example, God is spirit because, being pure act, he has no potency, and, hence, since material bodies have potential to change, he cannot have a material body.[9]

The case of Thomistic natural theology illustrates in yet another way the fact that our concept of God is tied to our analysis of causation. Thomas analyses causation in terms of act/potency categories. This basis in the act/potency distinction is also the reason why in Thomism, as Eric Mascall notes, the doctrine of analogy becomes an issue only after God's existence is proved. He states: 'the question of analogy does not arise at all in the mere proof of the existence of God; it arises only when, having satisfied ourselves that the existence of finite being declares its dependence upon self-existent being, we then

[7] See Anthony Kenny, *The Five Ways* (London, 1969), 24–33.
[8] Thomas Aquinas, *Summa Theologica*, ii (London, 1964), 13.
[9] Ibid. 23.

apprehend that no predicate can be attributed to finite being and to self-existent being univocally.'[10] Though pure actuality has no distinguishing characteristics, we must speak of it as if it did. We must use language whose very essence is to refer to composite beings, beings composed of form and matter in varying degrees of actuality and potentiality. The doctrine of analogical language attempts to overcome problems associated with the particular and peculiar Thomistic concept of God, the same concept which is the outcome of each of the Five Ways. This problem of reference is peculiar to Thomistic philosophy, and, for that reason, other articulations of a concept of God, based as they are on differing analyses of causality, may not face the same difficulties.

The connection between a concept of causality and the concept of God is crucial for understanding why Swinburne asserts in such a straightforward manner that God is a person. Since he begins with the concept of causal explanation, he only has two possible choices: persons and objects. It is by virtue of utilizing the concept of person as a cause that God is appropriately called a person.

We have seen how the concept of God as a person follows from the integrating power of the concept of personal agency. The conceptual connection between the concept of cause and the concept of God as a person, however, is seldom recognized.

This point is illustrated by considering the work of theologian, Maurice Wiles. Wiles's analysis of religious language reflects his prior understanding of the radical transcendence of divine reality. On his view, we cannot speak of God directly, and, thus, the language of faith uses images to serve as pointers to divine reality. He calls this a form of 'imaginative construction' or of 'symbolization'.[11] For example, our assertion that God created the world *ex nihilo* is a symbolization which points to the relationship between God and the world. The experience of ultimate dependence, the grasp of the ultimate objectivity in the experience of all-pervasive relativity, puts us into contact with divine reality. However, that rela-

---

[10] *Existence and Analogy* (London, 1949), 95.

[11] *Faith and the Mystery of God* (London, 1982), 18–19. This anthropological approach appears quite often in traditions influenced by Kant. Certain philosophers of religion appear to hold very similar positions. See the discussion on John Hick in ch. 8.

tionship of dependence is something, by virtue of its transcendent nature, which we cannot describe directly. Therefore, we must refer to it using symbols that point in its direction.

The vision of God's transcendence permeates Wiles's discussion of our affirmations about God in Christian doctrine. He explicates ideas, which are believed to be instances of the particularly Christian idea of God, God as Father or as creator *ex nihilo*, in light of it. However, this conception of God's transcendence creates a tension in his description of religious language. As Wiles understands the notion of God as creator, it is an imaginative construction articulating our experience of utter dependence. The expression 'creator' does not describe God, yet, on Wiles's view, it is cognitive.[12]

If we question why it is not descriptive, his response must be that God's reality transcends language. No language is adequate to describe God. But if this response itself is in question—that is, if we ask how Wiles knows that God's reality transcends language—the only response he has is to point back to the original experience of dependence. But *ex hypothesi* the experience itself does not tell us anything descriptive about the nature of the reality experienced and certainly not that God transcends our normal descriptive categories. Wiles's claim that the reality of God transcends our ordinary descriptive categories goes far beyond what is justified by the experience itself: it is an assertion about the nature of God.

This tension in Wiles's account of religious language reveals his confusion over the concept of God. He is nominally engaged in justifying the practice of theologizing in a post-natural-theology era. As he asks, 'If one rejects the possibility of arguing from premises about the world to conclusions about God but is still convinced that theology is a proper and necessary activity, what ways of proceeding are open?'[13] His answer is to reaffirm the experiential basis for knowledge of God. He states: 'Perhaps theology must after all abandon its claim to speak about the transcendent God; not in the paradoxical sense of becoming an atheistic theology, but in the sense that it will speak only of the effects of God as experienced, and make no attempt to speak of God in himself.'[14]

[12] Ibid. 17–30.   [13] *The Remaking of Christian Doctrine* (London, 1974), 23.
[14] Ibid. 25.

The problem with this account is that the assertion that God is radically transcendent assumes one concept of God, one akin to a classical view such as St Thomas's, and his experiential justification of belief in the existence of God assumes another, one which is fairly explicitly describable by the concept of person. Wiles attempts to bring the two concepts together with his analysis of religious language, but manages only to demonstrate their incompatibility.

The concept of God is an integrating concept: theism implies a single causal origin for the vast diversity of the universe. Wiles fails to recognize the limits which our language of causality places on our talk of God. To speak of God as radically transcendent implies that we know something about God. A Thomistic analysis of religious language accepts this paradox because its metaphysical analysis of 'being' entails the existence of a being of pure actuality. Wiles, however, rejects the traditional deductive proofs for God's existence, and, therefore, he cannot appeal to the same concepts which form the foundation of the traditional doctrine of analogy. Hence, when he speaks of God as a cause, the natural interpretation of his assertion is that he means to say straightforwardly that God is an agent. But if this is so, then Wiles is attempting to hold together two different and incompatible concepts of God. He cannot both hold his view of God's radical transcendence and also believe that God causes our religious experience.

Confusion about the conceptual connection between causality and the concept of God permeates philosophical as well as theological discussions about God. Anthony Flew, for example, shows complete insensitivity to this issue in his book, *God: A Critical Inquiry*.[15] In the preface he advocates 'Beginning from the Beginning' when analysing the justification for religious belief. By this phrase he means checking whether or not the concept of God is coherent before considering the question of God's existence. He comments:

The first task, therefore, before asking whether the relevant concept of God does in fact have application . . . is to explain the desired sense of the term 'God', and to show that what we have here is a coherent and possible concept which could truly be said to have application. It is

---

[15] (La Salle, Ill., 1984), first pub. as *God and Philosophy* (London, 1966).

only if and when this initial and traditionally evaded hurdle is satisfactorily overcome that we shall really be in a position to see how such
a Being could be identified, and what possible evidence is in fact
humanly attainable.[16]

Obviously the demand that we work with a coherent concept
is quite legitimate. It is a truth of logic that an incoherent
concept cannot be instantiated. The problem with Flew's
approach is that he fails to take account of differences in the
concept of God which come about as a consequence of differences in concepts of causality.

This is exemplified by his inclusion of both Thomistic
elements and elements of contemporary concepts of person in
the concept of God. Flew takes as an essential feature of any
account of theism that God is an agent with a will such that he
can be disobeyed.[17] Thus, Flew interprets agency along the
same lines as, for example, Swinburne. This interpretation, in
Flew's perspective, is necessary if God, in accordance with
ordinary piety, is to be personal. He then proceeds to query the
consistency of this notion with Thomistic ways of speaking of
God, namely that God is neither a member of a genus nor an
individual.[18] The problem with this manner of analysing the
concept of God is that it does justice to the integrity of neither
the Thomistic nor the contemporary ways of speaking of God.
It was not Thomas's intent to ascribe to God essential personhood of this kind. Thomistic natural theology, both recent and
medieval, describes God as pure Actuality, that in which
essence is identical with existence. His attributes, such as omnipotence, omniscience, and so on, are explicated in light of this
basic identification. It is from the fact that God is the metaphysical ground of the contingent universe that he is said to
create and, therefore, to be a person.[19] But calling God a person
is not intended in Thomism to attribute to God personhood in
the sense of the contemporary notion of person. The Thomistic
affirmation of God's immutability precludes ascribing to God
personhood in the modern sense. H. P. Owen comments:

If God is the Creator he must also be immutable in the sense that he
cannot change in any of his properties. He cannot be thus changed
either by a higher being (for there is no such being) or by his creatures

---

[16] Ibid. xi.   [17] Ibid. 23.   [18] Ibid. 29–30.
[19] H. P. Owen, *Christian Theism* (Edinburgh, 1984), 12.

(for they are totally dependent on and distinct from him). Moreover, if he exists necessarily he must actualize all his properties simultaneously; for in any entity existence and essence—*that* an entity is and *what* it is—are, though notionally distinguishable, ontologically inseparable.[20]

The Thomistic concept of immutability is incompatible with a contemporary notion of agency, and, therefore, it is not surprising that Flew finds incoherence. If, however, Thomism is considered as an integral system, Flew's complaints are not so evidently forceful.[21] For this reason more care must be taken when addressing the issue of the concept of God. It is not possible simply to object to the concept of God without also considering the sort of argument within which it is an integral part.

The concept of God as a person is thoroughly modern. The advantage of this concept is that it is anchored securely in our everyday conceptual framework.[22] Traditionally the contrast between God and creation requires using analogies to speak of God. As Swinburne has argued, the term 'person' must be used in its ordinary sense if we are to speak of God as a person in any meaningful way. There is a difference between language used to describe God and language used to describe ordinary human persons, but it is not in the meaning or application of language. What differs is how God manifests the attributes of being a person. Swinburne comments:

Although the theologian uses ordinary words to denote ordinary properties, he claims that the properties cited are manifested in unusual combinations and circumstances and to unusual degrees. God is a powerful person—but a very, very much more powerful person than any with whom we are ordinarily acquainted.[23]

At the basis of the different views on religious language are differing concepts of causality. Thomas, analysing causality in terms of the act/potency categories, requires some doctrine of analogy to speak of God. For Swinburne this is, for the most

---

[20] *Christian Theism*, p. 13.

[21] We consider the viability of a Thomistic alternative in ch. 8.

[22] I assume that Strawson has described reasonably accurately the 'actual structure of our thought about the world'. Hence, 'persons' and 'bodies' are part and parcel of our ordinary view of the world. See Strawson, *Individuals*, pt. 1.

[23] *The Coherence of Theism*, p. 51.

part, unnecessary.[24] The use of the concept of person to describe God needs no non-literal use of language since there is
nothing peculiar about the nature of God, along the lines of the
Thomistic concept of pure actuality, which requires it.

The concept of God as a person functions as an integrating
concept chiefly because it postulates a single personal causal
origin for the universe. However, as we noted above, other
features of the concept of person contribute to the integrative
power of theism. In the next section we shall examine the
concept of purposive activity as an additional integrative
feature of theism.

II

A world hypothesis explains by integrating the data of the
universe into a single coherent interpretive framework. Theistic systems such as Christianity or Islam postulate a personal
origin for the universe. But the origin of the universe is not the
only datum to be explained. This fact is, in essence, why Swinburne's strictly causal interpretation of the theistic hypothesis
is inadequate. World hypotheses, by contrast, must account for
other features of the universe also. One of these features is the
phenomenon of value. I include in this class phenomena such
as moral intuitions and a sense of the meaning of human life.
The universe does not wear on its sleeve, so to speak, the
answers to questions about moral right and wrong or about
whether there is any overall purpose to existence. World
hypotheses provide answers to questions of these kinds.

The concept of God as a person includes another integrative
feature which allows the data of value to be explained. Persons
are not only agents, but purposive ones also, and this purposive
feature of action supplies an additional integrative capacity for
theism. This is a corollary to the argument in the previous
section. God must be a person or an object, if it is to be said that
he brought about the universe. But if we speak of God as a
creative person, we imply also that God creates for some
reason, that is, in order to accomplish some purpose. Thus,
part of the explanatory power of theism is related to its ability

[24] He does use a concept of analogy but of a different kind. See *The Coherence of Theism*,
pp. 268–80. Cf. B. Mondin, *The Principle of Analogy in Protestant and Catholic Theology*
(The Hague, 1963).

to answer questions about morality and the ultimate meaning of the universe by reference to these purposes. In the minimal theism which Swinburne discusses, these purposes surface in theodicy. He appeals to the possibility of God purposively creating a world where rational creatures can mature in order to demonstrate the consistency of the existence of evil with an all-good, all-powerful God. But, since different theistic systems understand these purposes differently, an account of God's purposes is also a distinguishing criterion between sorts of theism. For example, Christian theism will derive its sense of God's purposes from the revelation present in the person of Jesus Christ, while Islam will centre its beliefs about the purposes of God around the Koran and the revelation spoken by Muhammad.

We can see how the will of God functions as an integrative concept by examining the problem of the relationship between moral obligation and God's commandments: 'Does God will the good because it is good; or are things good because God wills them?'[25] It is philosophically commonplace to say that religion as such has nothing to do with morality. Morality, it is claimed, is autonomous. God's will cannot be what makes an action morally right, for there are just some things that, in principle, no one could make right: things such as the wanton killing of innocent children. If God were to create a world where animate creatures indefinitely experienced extreme pain for no purpose, we could not say in any significant sense that he was good.[26]

In a broad sense, therefore, moral beliefs are independent of God's commands.[27] But there is also a sense in which a moral

---

[25] The problem is classically stated in Plato's *Euthyphro*. In the dialogue Socrates speaks of 'holiness' rather than goodness: 'Now think of this. Is what is holy holy because the gods approve it, or do they approve it because it is holy?' See *The Collected Dialogues of Plato*, ed. Edith Hamilton and Huntington Cairns (Princeton, NJ, 1961), 178. The problem has been generalized, however, to represent the problem of relating religion to morality. Cf. Paul Helm (ed.), *Divine Commands and Morality* (Oxford; 1981). This book contains a number of essays on this topic; see especially Helm's introduction.

[26] Swinburne, *The Coherence of Theism*, pp. 203–6.

[27] There are qualifications to this. Even if we were to admit that morality is autonomous, there would be, none the less, cases where, if God exists, we are obliged to do what he commands because of his relationship to us as creator. Thus, as children are obligated to obey their parents because of the parental relationship, so we are obligated to obey God because of the creator/created relationship. In this sense God is a source of moral obligation. See Swinburne, *The Coherence of Theism*, pp. 203–9.

judgement is justified in virtue of its relationship to a larger and more comprehensive understanding of what morality is about. Mitchell has argued that morality is 'essentially concerned with the fulfilment of men's needs as individuals and as members of society—with the necessary conditions of human well-being'.[28] If he is correct, we have a conception of morality which permits a significant explanatory relation between moral assertions and religion which does not compromise the autonomy of moral obligation. Religion supplies the conception of human well-being which guides moral discourse. Therefore, our specific intuitions about morality and human significance are explained by virtue of a broader view of the nature of man.

Swinburne, however, does not believe that morality can be used as evidence for theism at all. In his review of Mitchell's *Morality: Religious and Secular*, he comments:

But 'justification' in Mitchell's suggested moral argument is totally different from 'explanation' in the cosmological argument. If traditional morality cannot be justified, in Mitchell's view, then it would not be the true morality; our initial moral intuitions that it was the true morality would have been mistaken. The justification which traditional morality needs is to prove that it is the true morality. That is why the investigation needs other grounds for believing that there is a God before he can rationally believe that his supposed fact, that traditional morality is true, holds.[29]

But even if we consider morality to be autonomous, it can still constitute a body of 'facts' which can be explained by theism, so long as we bear in mind that it is not a sense of causal explanation that is intended. The point is that we have moral intuitions which are given and which stand as a plumb-line to gauge other beliefs and actions.[30] A religious system, or any world hypothesis, places these given intuitions into a framework which draws out their systematic interconnection to the needs of man and society. Though, being revisable, these intuitions lead only to prima facie beliefs, they also serve as a criterion for the adequacy of any metaphysical system. So any world hypothesis, be it Christian theism or some other

[28] *Morality: Religious and Secular* (Oxford, 1980), 107.
[29] *Journal of Theological Studies*, 32 (1981), 570.
[30] Mitchell, *Morality*, p. 98.

hypothesis, must save the phenomena of our moral intuitions, or be judged inadequate to the extent that it does not. It is this notion of 'saving the phenomena' which indicates how morality can be evidence for theism. Theism, inasmuch as it gives a coherent and complete analysis of our moral intuitions, is confirmed by the existence of just those intuitions.[31]

It is true, as Swinburne notes, that reasons can be given why particular moral intuitions ought to be discarded, but these reasons will form part of an alternative, competing metaphysical system which must be assessed in light of its inability to accept the prima facie force of these intuitions. Thus, there is an inevitable give and take in the argument. The explanatory relation is, again, one of integration. Theism as a world hypothesis explains why we have these particular moral intuitions and provides a rationale for having them. In the sense that morality exists as a phenomenon to be accounted for in these ways, theism provides us with one possible explanatory theory.

Some of the doctrines of Christian theism serve to illustrate this integrative explanatory function. Consider, for example, two central themes: the love of God and redemptive incarnation.[32] These do not exhaust the content of Christian belief, but they help distinguish Christian theism from other world hypotheses as well as from other sorts of theism.

Christian theology claims that God is love. If we seek a personal cause as an explanation for the existence of the universe, we are justified in speaking of God as a person. But it does not follow from the fact that God is personal that he will be loving. Swinburne, for example, argues that God is necessarily all-good: God, being omniscient, will know what the good thing to do is in each situation and, being omnipotent, will have no external forces to keep him from performing the good thing to do; hence, he will always do the good thing.[33] However, the idea that God is all-good in this sense, though portraying God's

---

[31] Cf. Stewart Sutherland, *God, Jesus and Belief: The Legacy of Theism* (Oxford, 1984), 16. He makes it a rule by which we can adjudicate between acceptable theologies. If a particular theology conflicts with our moral intuitions, so much the worse for the theology. Sutherland represents an extreme example of the claim that our moral beliefs can correct other of our beliefs.

[32] See Stephen Sykes, *The Identity of Christianity* (London, 1984). Everyone seems to agree that Christian theism must include some doctrines on the nature of God and the incarnation. But it remains very controversial how to interpret them.

[33] *The Coherence of Theism*, pp. 179–83; *The Existence of God*, pp. 97–102.

moral goodness accurately, falls short of the full Christian vision of God as love.

The distinction is due to the fact that to act lovingly toward someone is sometimes an act of supererogation. Always committing a good action in a situation is not always to do an act of love. For example, though we may pay a man his legitimate wage, we may refuse to do the loving thing which is to help him out of his debt by paying him more than his wage. God, in the Christian tradition, is not only morally perfect, he is also supremely loving. God by nature will not only do what is morally required, but will also do what is the most loving thing to do. The concept of love involves particular relational qualities such as caring, kindness, and self-sacrifice. Our closest analogies revolve around the loving relationships between parents and children. Parents love their children, both emotionally and demonstratively, through their provision and nurture. Similarly, we speak of God's provision for and nurture of his creation as aspects of his love for creation.

The Christian story yields several different images which illustrate the character of God's love. Among the parables in the Gospel accounts, one that illuminates God's character clearly is the parable of the prodigal son. The religious value of this parable is manifold.[34] Clearly it reveals something of the Christian vision of God. The paradigmatic illustration of this is the father's response to the lost son. In spite of the younger son's earlier rejection of his family, the father joyously welcomes him back. And, as the father in the parable received back with forgiveness and joy his son, so God welcomes with forgiveness and joy those who are separated from him.

The concept of God as a loving person is certainly not unique to Christian theism. Other theistic traditions speak of God's love in no less unequivocal terms than Christian theism. What uniquely identifies Christianity is the mode of God's self-giving love. Christianity claims that the supreme revelation of the character of God is Jesus. Here we approach the Christian idea of redemptive incarnation.[35] Implicit in the parable is the idea

[34] See Joachim Jeremias, *The Parables of Jesus*, trans. S. H. Hooke (New York, 1955), 103–6.

[35] The doctrines of the atonement and incarnation are the subject of much debate in current literature. Cf. F. W. Dillestone, *The Christian Understanding of the Atonement* (London, 1968), with Wiles, *The Remaking of Christian Doctrine*, ch. 4. On the

that something separates God from man. The son's separation from his family is a picture of the problem of sin.[36] Man offends against God's law and receives as punishment the severing of the divine relationship. For the Christian sin is a deeply rooted problem which he cannot correct himself. The character of God's self-giving love is demonstrated by God's initiative to overcome the problem. The focus of this initiative is the life, death, and resurrection of Jesus. In the Fourth Gospel we find summarized the traditional description of God's loving action: 'For God so loved the world that he gave his only Son, that whoever believes in him should not perish but have eternal life.'[37] This passage captures the notion that the love of God moved him to action, that is, to send his Son so that the separation could be overcome. Jesus, therefore, is the locus of redemption and revelation: redemption, because through his death and resurrection man is reconciled to God, and revelation, because through the giving of his life we see God as he truly is.

The integrative capacity of this picture of God is twofold. One, God's purposes for creation are related to man's relationship to God. God creates man in order that a divine–human communion can take place. This aspect of God's purposes forms a part of man's *telos* and helps define man's ultimate significance in the universe. But this explanatory function is enhanced by a second aspect of this concept of God. The Christian picture of God is also a picture of man. Christian doctrine declares that man is made in the 'image of God'. The doctrine of the *Imago Dei*, though interpreted in many different ways, transfers the image of God's self-giving character directly to man. Since God's character is defined in terms of self-giving love, man's existence ought also to be characterized as a life of self-giving love. Interpreted in terms of the explanatory power of theism as a world hypothesis, this feature of Christian doctrine promotes a specific view of human well-being.

incarnation see John Hick (ed.), *The Myth of God Incarnate* (London, 1977). This book has elicited a great deal of discussion. Cf. Michael Green (ed.), *The Truth of God Incarnate* (London, 1977), Michael Goulder (ed.), *Incarnation and Myth* (London, 1979), and A. E. Harvey (ed.), *God Incarnate: Story and Belief* (London, 1981).

[36] Basil Mitchell, 'How the Concept of Sin is Related to Moral Wrongdoing', *Religious Studies*, 20 (1984), 165–73.

[37] John 3: 16 (RSV).

Given this conception of morality, we can see how a world hypothesis explains moral values. It provides a picture of what human well-being is, and the picture guides discussion of what is morally right or wrong. Thus, Christianity, taking the love of God and the example of Jesus as the key, puts high value on the centrality of God-like love for a well-lived human life.[38] Not every world hypothesis, however, has the same 'picture' as Christian theism, and thus moralities based on them can be correlatively different. For example, one version of a materialist world hypothesis is expressed in the moral stance of the existentialist Jean-Paul Sartre. In his view man has no nature, but is the summation of his historical experience. This position leads Sartre to a view of human well-being which discards traditional moral intuitions and leads to a conception of morality which is radically individualistic: what is right is simply what a person chooses.[39]

In this chapter I have argued that the explanatory power of the concept of God as a person as an integrative concept is not exhausted by the idea of God as a cause. The theistic world hypothesis includes the capacity to answer questions of ultimacy and meaning, and the strength of any theistic world hypothesis for this function revolves around its account of God's purposes for creation. We see this integrative capacity exhibited in a theistic system such as Christianity. God's existence explains how the universe and all that it contains came about, but it also explains why the universe is ordered as such to produce free creatures such as human beings. Such a system also explains why traditional moral intuitions are so deeply ingrained in our society, and why we value acts of love, of supererogatory self-sacrifice.

These two integrating functions serve to illustrate how a metaphysical world hypothesis 'makes sense of' the data of the universe. Two very different aspects of existence, the givenness of the physical universe and the phenomena of morality and the sense of human significance, are integrated into a single coherent picture represented in this case by Christian theism. Though Swinburne's conception of the

[38] Mitchell, *Morality: Religious and Secular*, pp. 122–37.
[39] Mary Warnock, *Existential Ethics* (London, 1967), 29.

theistic hypothesis addresses the first of these concerns, it ignores the second.

These two features of existence, however, are not the only data which theism as a world hypothesis explains. Theism provides an explanation for the existence of every contingent thing in the universe in a sense which goes beyond the fact that God is the cause of the universe. That God should have this kind of ultimacy requires that he should be a logically necessary being. In the next chapter, I shall explore what this means.

7

NECESSITY AND EXPLANATION

I HAVE examined the integrative capacity of the concept of God as a person. A further feature of the concept of God which contributes to its integrative power is the idea that God is a necessary being. Theists frequently describe God in terms of necessity, but they have conflicting views on just what God's necessity amounts to. The sense of necessity which I think is important for the integrative explanatory power of theism is logical necessity. Thus, when I say that God is a necessary being, I mean to say that God exists by logical necessity. That is to say, any logically possible world includes God.[1]

Discussion of the necessity of God's existence is typically part of an analysis of the ontological argument. This is unfortunate because it ignores the power of the hypothesis of the existence of a logically necessary God to answer questions about the ultimate nature of existence, questions such as 'Why is there something rather than nothing?' In this chapter I shall argue that the concept of a logically necessary God has explanatory power and, therefore, adds significant weight to the theistic hypothesis.

Swinburne, along with many other philosophers, rejects as incoherent the description of God as a logically necessary being. However, he admits that ultimately the only proof which can be given for the coherence of the concept of God itself is an inductive argument that establishes the likelihood of the existence of God: if God exists, then the concept of God must be coherent. It is plausible, therefore, to argue that if the concept of God as logically necessary plays an important explanatory role in the theistic world hypothesis, this gives reason to believe that the concept of logically necessary existence is coherent.

---

[1] This is a preliminary description. I discuss the concept of a logically necessary being in more detail in Section II below. In this chapter I do not distinguish between the concept of a logically necessary being and the concept of a being that exists by logical necessity.

I

Traditional language about God's necessity suggests that God has been taken to be a logically necessary being. Leibniz, for example, states:

if there is a reality in essences or in possibilities or indeed in the eternal truths, this reality is based upon something existent and actual, and, consequently, in the existence of the necessary Being in whom essence includes existence or in whom possibility is sufficient to produce actuality.... Therefore God alone (or the Necessary Being) has this prerogative that if he be possible he must necessarily exist, and, as nothing is able to prevent the possibility of that which involves no bounds, no negation, and consequently, no contradiction, this alone is sufficient to establish *a priori* his existence.[2]

It is clear that Leibniz meant something akin to logical necessity. He believes, for example, that the ontological argument is valid, but that it simply needs to be augmented by demonstrating that God is indeed a logically possible being. If God is possible, Leibniz argues, he exists.[3] Further, he uses God's absolute, or metaphysical, necessity in the cosmological argument to satisfy the principle of sufficient reason. Swinburne, commenting on Leibniz's cosmological argument, says:

Leibniz has ... deployed the principle of sufficient reason as a metaphysically necessary truth. The principle boils down to the claim that everything not metaphysically necessary has an explanation in something metaphysically necessary. A being has metaphysical necessity according to Leibniz, if from its 'essence existence springs'; i.e. if it could not but exist.[4]

The principle of sufficient reason is satisfied by the existence of God because God's existence 'springs' from his essence in a logically necessary way: it is of the essence of God that he exists.

For Thomistic arguments, the existence of composite beings raises the question of God's existence. The metaphysical requirement for the existence of composite beings entails the

[2] G. F. W. Leibniz, *Discourse on Metaphysics*, trans. G. R. Montgomery (La Salle, Ill., 1927), cited in Lewis White Beck (ed.), *Eighteenth Century Philosophy* (New York, 1966), 200.

[3] *New Essays Concerning Human Understanding*, appendix 10, in John Hick (ed.), *The Existence of God* (London, 1964), 37–9. See also Nicholas Rescher, *Leibniz: An Introduction to His Philosophy* (Oxford, 1979), 146–7.

[4] *The Existence of God*, p. 127.

existence of a being that is not composite, one whose essence is identical with its existence. This being, as Thomas reminds us, is commonly called God.[5]

The Thomistic metaphysical analysis requires that actual existence precede potential existence.[6] Any actual existence in this world, or any possible world, because it is composite, requires for its constant 'actualization' a being that is not composite, namely, God. No possible world that does not include God could be actual.[7] Therefore, since nothing can come about without God's also keeping it in existence, nothing, in Thomas's view, is truly possible if God does not exist. This metaphysical fact about existence is consonant with interpreting Thomas's concept of God in terms of logical necessity. For Thomas (and Leibniz) the set of possible worlds which contain God is coextensive with the set of all possible worlds. Therefore, it would be wrong to drive a sharp wedge between logical necessity and the necessity attaching to a being of pure act.[8]

This conclusion is confirmed by the way the necessity of

[5] There is debate over whether or not the principle of sufficient reason is implied in fact in Thomas's Five Ways. Copleston, for example, suggests that the proofs are based on the 'fact that everything must have its sufficient reason, the reason why it exists' (*A History of Philosophy*, vol. ii, pt. 2 (New York, 1962), 64–5). William Lane Craig, however, contests this. He contends that Thomas bases the arguments on a principle of causality rather than on a principle of sufficient reason. See *The Cosmological Argument from Plato to Leibniz*, chs. 5 and 9.

[6] Keith Ward, *Rational Theology and the Creativity of God* (Oxford, 1982), 17–22. Ward gives a number of other reasons in support of his interpretation of Thomas. I believe his interpretation is substantially correct.

[7] Therefore I think Geach is incorrect in his assessment of Thomas's view of necessity. If he is correct in the use of the term 'necessity', then he is incorrect in the sense that what distinguishes God from angels is something beyond necessity. This 'beyond' I call logical necessity. Thus we may distinguish between modern uses and Scholastic uses of the term 'necessity'. See P. T. Geach and G. E. M. Anscombe, *Three Philosophers* (Oxford, 1967), 115–16. Cf. Patterson Brown, 'St. Thomas' Doctrine of Necessary Being', *Philosophical Review*, 73 (1964), 76–90.

[8] In contrast cf. John Hick, 'A Critique of the Second Argument', in John Hick and Arthur C. McGill (eds.), *The Many-Faced Argument* (London, 1968). In personal conversation Swinburne has taken exception to my conclusion here. He finds it problematic to speak of Thomistic arguments using modern modal notions. To his mind there is simply too great a gap between Scholastic arguments and modern ontological arguments. I agree that it is a complex and difficult task to understand the relation between Scholastic and modern thought, but the task is not impossible, and I believe, for the reasons stated, that we can come to some fairly strong conclusions. A recent argument against this position is Kenneth Surin, 'Theistic Arguments and Rational Theism', *International Journal for Philosophy of Religion*, 16 (1984), 123–5.

God's existence functions in traditional arguments, both philo-sophical and theological. If by definition God is a necessary being, in the sense of logical necessity, cosmological questions simply do not arise with respect to God. His existence is self-explanatory in a way that the existence of no other being is. The factual existence of a necessary being answers the question 'Why something rather than nothing?'.[9]

God's logically necessary existence also distinguishes him from any other kind of being. Leibniz, for example, argues that the world could not have this kind of absolute or metaphysical necessity: 'For the present world is necessary physically or hypothetically, but not absolutely or meta-physically . . . and so there must exist something different from the plurality of beings, that is the world, which, as we have allowed and have shown, is not of metaphysical neces-sity.'[10] Anselm, describing God as 'that than which no greater could be conceived', derives from that description God's logically necessary existence.[11] The point is that, for both Anselm and Leibniz, what uniquely identifies God is or entails his logical necessity.

The theological role of necessity relates to this sense of God's ultimacy. The theological doctrine of creation points to God as the source of all existence: nothing could exist except through his agency.[12] A weaker sense of necessity might be consistent with this religious intuition, but it seems more adequate, as a description of God, to attribute to him abso-lute ultimacy, that is, not only ultimacy in this world, but ultimacy in every possible world.[13]

[9] Necessity is taken here in the modern sense, not the Scholastic sense.

[10] 'On the Ultimate Origination of Things' in *The Philosophical Writings of Leibniz*, trans. Mary Morris (London, 1934), 33.

[11] God's perfection is the basis for Anselm's claim that God is such that 'no greater can be conceived'. The perfection of God, therefore, distinguishes God from, among other things, Gaunilo's lost island. See John Hick, 'Gaunilo and Anselm' in Hick and McGill (eds.), *The Many-Faced Argument*, p. 23 n.

[12] I make this claim on the basis of the sense of God's absoluteness which permeates the Biblical literature. See Mascall's commentary on Exodus 3:14, in *Existence and Analogy*, pp. 13–14. Cf. also Owen, *Christian Theism*, pp. 9–26. He begins his discussion with the doctrine of creation.

[13] Cf. Anthony O'Hear's discussion of the religious intuition which lies behind the ontological argument in *Experience, Explanation and Faith*, pp. 143–85. He notes: 'But it does seem possible that those who would put God beyond being and conceptualization, and those who are attracted to the reasoning underlying the ontological argument are

Swinburne, in contrast to the tradition, explicitly denies that God is logically necessary. He explains God's necessary existence, as he conceives it, in this way: to say that God is a necessary being is 'to say that the existence of God is a brute fact which is inexplicable—not in the sense that we do not know its explanation, but in the sense that it does not have one—it is a terminus of complete explanation'.[14] God is a necessary being because he is the ultimate brute fact: God simply has no explanation.[15] This concept of necessity, he believes, captures the sense of ultimacy and independence appropriate to God. God is not dependent on anything 'the description of which is not entailed by' his existence.[16]

One consequence of this definition is that necessity is predicated of whatever is the 'brute fact' of the universe. Swinburne states: 'If there is no God or any similar being, "the universe exists" would be a necessary proposition. For in that case the universe would not depend for its existence on anything else. The existence of the universe would be an ultimate brute fact.'[17]

A further consequence of this definition of necessity is that God's necessity is not relevant to the explanatory power of theism. In traditional arguments for God's existence, the logical necessity of God provided the means to halt the regress of sufficient reasons. But, by Swinburne's definition, the concept of necessity can have no relevance to the question of God's existence. In fact the description of anything as the necessary being of the universe is simply a recognition that it is the brute fact of existence.

If we take Leibniz and Thomas as representatives of the theistic tradition, it is obvious that Swinburne's definition of necessity does not represent the meaning of the traditional claims about God's necessity. The sense of necessity in both Leibnizian and Thomistic concepts of God is similar, if not

trying to express much the same thought: that God has a type of existence which is totally beyond what is possessed by any created thing, and that created things are less real than absolute being and have reality only "in so far as they have their being from God" and "remain in him", as St Augustine puts it (*Confessions* VII, 11)' (p. 147). Illtyd Trethowan makes a similar sort of claim in 'The Significance of Process Theology', *Religious Studies*, 19 (1983), 311–22.

[14] *The Existence of God*, pp. 92–3.   [15] i.e. God has no causal explanation.
[16] *The Coherence of Theism*, pp. 250–1.   [17] Ibid.

identical, to logical necessity. In so far as he is not concerned so much with living up to tradition as with having a coherent concept, the changes Swinburne makes are understandable. But it is worth noting that, though he affirms God's necessary existence, his concept of necessity neither uniquely identifies God nor plays a role in his argument which is in any way similar to that which it plays in traditional thought.

II

The description of God as a logically necessary being is a contentious description. For example, in his debate with Copleston, Russell, following in the tradition of Hume and Kant, stipulates that logical necessity is solely the property of propositions and, therefore, concludes that God cannot be a logically necessary being.[18]

The notion that God is a logically necessary being cannot be separated from the idea that God, in the strongest possible sense, is conceived of as a perfect being, i.e. the ultimate source of existence, the supremely valuable being in the universe, and the 'adequate object of religious worship' (hereafter I shall refer to this as God's ultimacy).[19] Swinburne, characterizing this ultimacy, speaks of God as the 'personal ground of being'. Anselm, also trying to capture this sense of God's absoluteness, describes God as 'that than which no greater can be conceived'. The motivation for claiming that God is a logically necessary being stems from the conviction that God is necessarily the ultimate being in the universe. The reason anyone countenances the possibility of the claim that God is logically necessary is in this connection. If such a being is possible, and if God is not identical with that being, then God would not have the ultimacy appropriate to his nature.

Anselm's articulation of the ontological argument presupposes the perfection of God. Anselm has been criticized for making existence a property of perfection, and, if the criticisms voiced by Hume and Kant are correct, then his way of stating

[18] Russell and Copleston, 'The Debate', pp. 168–72.

[19] This is my attempt to articulate the point made in the previous section with reference to Leibniz and Anselm. Cf. J. N. D. Findlay's discussion of the 'religiously adequate object of worship' in 'Can God's Existence be Disproved?', *Mind*, 52 (1948), 108–18.

what it means to be 'that than which no greater can be conceived' is surely mistaken. However, others have suggested that Anselm's categories are not the only categories that can express God's logical necessity.

It is a virtue of Plantinga's treatment of the ontological argument that he expresses God's ultimacy in terms of logical necessity without slipping into the same problems as Anselm. He describes his version of the ontological argument as 'a victorious modal version'.[20] Mackie, taking exception to Plantinga's self-description, comments:

This argument, then, is not only 'not a successful piece of natural theology', but is not even in any sense 'victorious': there is no rival view over which it is victorious, or which it can be plausibly said to defeat. In fact a plausible system of modal logic and possible worlds would either reject the world-indexing of properties or else adopt nested sets of possible worlds and so resist the collapsing of iterated modalities into their final members. With either of these amendments, Plantinga's argument would not get off the ground. But even if we accept the rather arbitrary modal system which makes it valid, we have no good reason to accept rather than to reject its key premise. Altogether, then, the argument is worthless as a support for theism, and is interesting mainly as a logical peculiarity.[21]

Plantinga could well agree that his argument does not support theism; indeed, as Mackie points out, Plantinga accepts that the ontological argument is not a successful piece of natural theology. However, to understand what Plantinga accomplishes, we must first remember the context from which the typical objections to the ontological argument come. Kant, for example, argues not only that the ontological argument does not work but that it is not even an argument. According to Kant, the argument is based on an improperly formed sentence, one that makes existence a predicate.[22] As it stands, Kant's criticism rejects the very statement of the argument. Plantinga's restatement—and the reason it can be described as

[20] *The Nature of Necessity*, p. 213. See also Alvin Plantinga, *God, Freedom and Evil* (Grand Rapids, Mich., 1978), 111.

[21] *The Miracle of Theism*, p. 62.

[22] Cf. Immanuel Kant, *The Critique of Pure Reason*, trans. Norman Kemp Smith (New York, 1965), 200–7; G. E. Moore, 'Is Existence a Predicate?', *Proceedings of the Aristotelian Society*, Supplement 15 (1936), 175–88. See also Jonathan Barnes, *The Ontological Argument* (London, 1972), 39 ff.

victorious—side-steps these traditional objections to its formulation. Mackie may believe that Plantinga's modal system
is peculiar, but he cannot, and does not, accuse Plantinga, as
Kant accuses the traditional formulations of the argument, of
complete conceptual confusion.

Plantinga provides a cogent alternative interpretation of the
ontological argument based not on the concepts of existence
and perfection, but on the notion of possible worlds. God's
absolute ultimacy, and his logical necessity, are defined in
terms of existing in all logically possible worlds. By approach-
ing the concept of God this way he intends to take what is
cogent in the traditional arguments and to leave behind the
problems associated with the particular conceptuality of
Anselm's original statement. Thus, rather than construing
existence as a perfection of the most perfect being, Plantinga
uses the concepts of maximal excellence and maximal
greatness. A maximally excellent being is one who has omniscience, omnipotence, and moral perfection. A maximally
great being is one who possesses the property of being
maximally excellent in all logically possible worlds. God is
maximally excellent, but, because he is the absolutely ultimate
being, he will also be maximally great, that is, if a maximally
great being is possible.[23] Therefore, the claim that God is a
logically necessary being presupposes that maximal greatness
is possible and that, this being so, God is maximally great. The
issue, as Plantinga admits, boils down to the question of the
possibility of a maximally great being.

By defining the concept of God using the notions of maximal
greatness and possible worlds, Plantinga's argument is victorious because it does not lead to the problems of formulation
attendant on Anselm's understanding of God's logical necessity. He concludes:

What shall we say of these arguments? Clearly they are valid; and
hence they show that if it is even possible that God, so thought of,
exists, then it is true and necessarily true that he does. The only
question of interest, it seems to me, is whether its main premise—that
indeed unsurpassable greatness is possibly exemplified, that there is
an essence entailing unsurpassable greatness—is true.[24]

---

[23] Plantinga, *The Nature of Necessity*, pp. 214–15.   [24] Ibid. 216–17.

Plantinga admits that one of the main premises is not obviously true, and, hence, the argument is not successful as an argument for the existence of God. He would agree with Mackie's assessment that his use of a particular system of modal logic and of the concept of world-indexed properties leads him to his conclusion.[25] But Plantinga does prove that the argument is valid, and this is enough to render Mackie's objection superfluous. Plantinga's restatement expresses very elegantly the belief that God is the ultimate being in the universe.

Of course the epistemic question remains: how do we know whether God is possible, and hence actual, or that such a being is impossible? Mackie questions whether it is reasonable to believe that God is possible, and his question is important for what it reveals. Mackie recognizes that, even if the ontological argument is valid, some other way is needed to show that it is sound. In this respect he appears to agree, at least implicitly, with Thomas, who concluded thus:

I maintain . . . that the proposition 'God exists' is self-evident in itself, for . . . its subject and predicate are identical, since God is his own existence. But, because what it is to be God is not evident to us, the proposition is not self-evident to us, and needs to be made evident. This is done by means of things which, though less evident in themselves, are nevertheless more evident to us, by means, namely, of God's effects.[26]

This discussion clarifies to some extent what it means to claim that God is a logically necessary being. God is a logically necessary being if God is, in Plantinga's terms, either maximally great, or, in terms mentioned earlier in this section, the ultimate being of the universe.

Swinburne discusses two objections to the possibility of God's being logically necessary. He first considers and rejects Russell's objection that logical necessity is solely a property of propositions and not things. He responds to this objection by providing particular counter-examples such as numbers. For example, the existence of a prime number between 9 and 13 illustrates the fact that some things do exist by logical

[25] See G. E. Hughes and M. J. Cresswell, *An Introduction to Modal Logic* (London, 1968), pt. 1.
[26] *Summa Theologica*, p. 7.

necessity. There is a prime number between 9 and 13, namely 11, and it exists by logical necessity. That is, there are no possible worlds where the number 11 does not exist. Though, admittedly the importance of this sort of example is limited—since God is not exactly like a number—it does demonstrate that our language contains propositions which state the existence of logically necessary things.[27] And, any attempt, Swinburne concludes, to make the principle—only propositions are logically necessary—include these sorts of counter-examples and also exclude beings such as God has so far proved elusive. Thus, this objection, to Swinburne's mind, gives no reason for rejecting the idea and possibility of God's existing by logical necessity.

He argues, however, that a second, more substantive, objection is conclusive. If God is a logically necessary being, then any proposition entailed by the proposition stating his existence will itself be logically necessary. In the case of God's logically necessary existence, however, this leads to extremely counter-intuitive results. For example, the proposition 'God exists' entails the proposition 'There is a non-embodied person' (since God is a spirit). Therefore, if the proposition 'God exists' is logically necessary, so is the proposition 'There is a non-embodied person'. And if the latter proposition is logically necessary, its negation is logically impossible.[28] It follows then that the proposition 'All persons are embodied' is logically impossible. Yet, according to Swinburne, the proposition 'All persons are embodied' seems to be coherent, i.e. seems to be possible. 'Of course,' he comments, 'there just might be contradictions buried in the statements which we have been considering, but in the absence of argument to the contrary we ought to assume what clearly appears to be the case that there are no such buried contradictions, and so that ["God exists"] is

[27] J. C. A. Gaskin admits that these examples do illustrate necessary existential truths, but believes this is contrary to the sort of being God is. God is not a number nor a concept. He concludes, therefore, that these examples do not help the theist clarify what they mean by God's logically necessary existence. See *Hume's Philosophy of Religion* (London, 1978), 62–3. I agree with Gaskin that God is not a number nor simply a concept; but this does not seem to negate the point of the examples, namely, that there is nothing conceptually incongruous in asserting logically necessary existential propositions.

[28] *The Coherence of Theism*, p. 265.

not logically necessary. Atheism is a coherent supposition.'[29] Thus, he concludes, God is not a logically necessary being.

His general premiss in this argument is indubitably correct: propositions entailed by a logically necessary proposition must also be logically necessary. And it seems correct to say that, if God exists necessarily, there are no possible worlds where only embodied persons exist. But Swinburne draws from that implication the conclusion that God cannot be logically necessary. This conclusion is much stronger than his argument can actually support.

Swinburne's test for coherence contains two contrasting elements. With the first, which I shall call the deductive test, he tries to demonstrate the incoherence of the proposition 'God is a logically necessary being'. This, as we saw above, involves deducing a further proposition which is then tested for its coherence. If the entailment proves to be incoherent, then the original proposition is also incoherent. With the second element he tests the coherence of the entailment. Here he uses the 'obvious-contradiction' test. Unless there is an obvious contradiction in a proposition, then we are entitled to take the proposition to be coherent. With the second test, he concludes that the proposition 'All persons are embodied' is coherent. And using the first test, since the coherence of 'All persons are embodied' entails the incoherence of 'God is logically necessary', he concludes that the latter proposition must be incoherent.

Each of these methods has some intuitive plausibility. But a question remains whether their use in this context can prove the incoherence of the proposition that God is a logically necessary being. The problem is that Swinburne's argument invites a *tu quoque* response. If he used the deductive method to prove the incoherence of the proposition 'All persons are embodied' and tested the coherence of the implication by seeking an obvious contradiction, then he could just as cogently prove that it is logically impossible that all persons are embodied. The proposition 'All persons are embodied' entails the proposition 'No persons are non-embodied'. Thus, if the proposition 'All persons are embodied' is coherent, then its logical entailment 'No persons are non-embodied' will also be coherent.

[29] Ibid.

However, the entailment 'No persons are non-embodied' is inconsistent with propositions such as 'The maximally great being loves everyone'.

By definition the concept 'maximally great being' entails that there is at least one non-embodied person in every logically possible world. Hence, either the proposition 'The maximally great being loves everyone' is coherent and the proposition 'No persons are non-embodied' is not; or the proposition 'No persons are non-embodied' is coherent, and the proposition 'The maximally great being loves everyone' is not. But the concepts in the proposition 'The maximally great being loves everyone' are not obviously contradictory, that is, there is no obvious contradiction in the assertion that a maximally great being loves everyone. Hence, recalling Swinburne's argument above, though there may be a buried contradiction, until that is proved, it is reasonable to assume that the proposition 'The maximally great being loves everyone' is coherent and the proposition 'All persons are embodied' is not.

What seems unreasonable about his method is that it is far too lenient. Since it is more difficult to prove that a contradiction exists, it allows virtually any entailment to be coherent and to count against the possibility that God is logically necessary. Furthermore, if Swinburne used the 'obvious-contradiction' test on the proposition that God is a maximally great being, that proposition would turn out coherent also. If he weakened his demand with respect to the proposition 'God is a logically necessary being' or strengthened his demand with respect to the proposition 'All persons are embodied', he would be forced to admit that neither proposition, given these particular tests, can be shown to be incoherent. Thus, the most he can say is that either 'God is a logically necessary being' is possible or 'All persons are embodied' is possible, but that both cannot be.

Even if the concepts of 'person' or 'embodiment' in propositions such as 'All persons are embodied' are internally consistent with each other, it would not show that those propositions are coherent. A proposition can be logically impossible for reasons other than the internal incoherence of the concepts used to state it. Keith Ward, in examining a similar proposition, makes this point in this way:

At first, . . . it seems strange to say that 'No being exists which knows more than I do' is self-contradictory. Taken on its own, of course, it does not contradict itself. It is necessarily false, not because the phrase contains a self-contradiction, but because it contradicts another assertion which is necessarily true, namely, 'There is an omniscient being', and that the latter phrase is entailed by one that is necessarily true; it is not enough simply to look hard at the statement itself. . . . To say that 'God exists' is logically necessary is not to trivialize the concept of God by making his existence a matter of verbal definition. 'God exists' is not made true by an arbitrary set of axioms. It is made true by the existence of God, and what makes it non-contingent is that there is no possible world in which God does not exist.[30]

Ward's point is this. The impossibility which attaches to propositions like 'No being exists which knows more than I do' or 'All persons are embodied' cannot appropriately be evaluated by examining the concepts of person and embodiment, and, for that reason, Swinburne's argument fails to show that the concept of God as a logically necessary being is impossible.

Swinburne believes that the logical possibility of 'All persons are embodied' depends on the lack of an internal contradiction in the concepts. But the impossibility involved is not a consequence of a contradiction between the concept of person and embodiment. The contradiction involves predicating the property 'being embodied' of all the persons which exist in a particular logically possible world. Our linguistic conventions permit us to predicate of persons, as an accidental property, both embodiment and non-embodiment. But we cannot determine the possible extension of these concepts in a possible world by examining just the concepts themselves. In any possible world the term 'person' will pick out all those objects which are persons. If God's existence is logically necessary, then there is no world where the concept 'all persons' does not pick out God. Therefore, on this view, since every possible world includes at least one non-embodied person, the contradiction which makes propositions such as 'All persons are embodied' logically impossible occurs at the point of predicating the property of 'being embodied' of every person which exists in that particular possible world. That is to say, the

<hr>

[30] *Rational Theology*, pp. 43–4.

proposition 'All persons are embodied' is logically necessarily false not because the concepts of 'person' and 'embodiment' are internally inconsistent but because, given the existence of a maximally great being, the concept 'all persons' picks out a non-embodied person in every possible world. Swinburne's mistake is to assume that, because a statement contains concepts which are internally consistent, it describes a truly possible state of affairs.

Swinburne's argument against the possibility of God being logically necessary fails, therefore, on two counts. In the first place, he inconsistently applies the various tests for coherence and incoherence, which leads to a question about what his argument actually proves. Both propositions 'God is a logically necessary being' and 'All persons are embodied' have no obvious contradictions, and each of them entails the impossibility of propositions which have no obvious contradictions. The correct conclusion to draw is that his test shows that not both of the propositions can be possible, though we cannot show which is the impossible one. In the second place, there is a question about what the apparent coherence of the proposition 'All persons are embodied' demonstrates. Even if the internal consistency of the concepts which make up the proposition 'All persons are embodied' is granted, it is not evident that it would show the impossibility of the proposition 'God is a logically necessary being'.

There is, as we saw earlier, another test for logical possibility which may prove more helpful in determining the coherence of God's logically necessary existence. If one can, from factual premises, show that a proposition is probably true, then this constitutes a coherence proof for it, since a proposition must be coherent to be true.[31] It may be the case that this method is more appropriate for deciding the coherence of the concept of a maximally great being than the other method.

Two questions, however, can be raised concerning this method of determining the coherence of 'God is maximally great'. First, though Swinburne, in fact, concedes that the only way to prove satisfactorily the coherence of the concept of God is to prove that God exists, it is not obvious which concept of God a proof of his existence would show to be coherent: that

---

[31] Swinburne, *The Coherence of Theism*, pp. 45–9.

God is a maximally excellent being or that God is a maximally great being. And secondly, Swinburne gives a third argument against speaking of God as a logically necessary being: a logically necessary being, he argues, cannot explain a logically contingent universe. If his argument is correct, it is questionable whether any argument could be taken as a proof of the coherence of the proposition 'God is a logically necessary being'. In the next section, therefore, I shall address the issue of how a logically necessary God can serve as an explanation.

III

Swinburne affirms the logical contingency of God's existence because of problems concerning the explanatory relation between logically necessary and logically contingent propositions. He states:

Nor can anything logically necessary provide any explanation of anything logically contingent. For a full explanation is . . . such that the *explanandum* (i.e. the phenomenon requiring explanation) is deducible from it. But you cannot deduce anything logically contingent from anything logically necessary. And a partial explanation is in terms of something which in the context makes the occurrence of the *explanandum* probable, without which things would probably have gone some other (logically possible) way. Yet a world in which some logically necessary truth did not hold is an incoherent supposition, not one in which things would probably have gone some other way. These are among many reasons why it must be held that God is a logically contingent being, although maybe one necessary in some other ways.[32]

The force of his observation lies in the obvious fact that something logically contingent cannot be deduced from something logically necessary. Prima facie examples of this truth abound. From a tautology such as 'All bachelors are unmarried males' contingent truths such as 'John is a bachelor' cannot be deduced. The colour of the paper on which I write, a contingent fact, does not follow from the necessary truth that red is a colour. This rule seems clearly true.

The question, then, is in what respect it applies to the issue of God's logical necessity. There is a contingent universe

[32] *The Existence of God*, p. 76.

which needs explaining, and, by Swinburne's judgement, God's existence best explains it. However, if God is logically necessary, his existence cannot explain something contingent like the universe. If God were logically necessary, then that which is deduced from the fact that he exists, namely, the universe, itself would be logically necessary. But, in his view, the possibility of explanation rests on the possibility that one thing would occur rather than another. If the universe exists by logical necessity, it could not be other than it is and, for that reason, would not be more liable for explanation than, say, a prime number; but if the universe could truly have been different—or even not at all—then either it does not exist by logical necessity or a logically necessary truth does not hold. Since it is incoherent to suppose that there is a possible world where a logical truth does not hold, the universe must not exist by logical necessity.

Two aspects of the argument can be separated from one another. First, Swinburne argues that a logically contingent proposition cannot be deduced from a logically necessary one; and secondly, he argues that a logically necessary being cannot cause a logically contingent universe. As I see it, the first conclusion is true, but the second is not. The issue concerns the nature of the logically necessary being and whether it is his logical necessity which is involved in the causal explanation of the universe.

It is important to put Swinburne's discussion into context. He has developed his understanding of causal explanation carefully and has identified a number of other kinds of explanation. Complete explanation, for example, is a special case of full explanation. He says: 'A complete explanation of the occurrence of E is a full explanation of its occurrence in which all the factors cited are such that there is no explanation (either full or partial) of their existence or operation in terms of factors operative at the time of their existence or operation.'[33] Yet a further sort of explanation he calls ultimate explanation: 'I define an ultimate explanation of E as a complete explanation of E, in which the factors C and R cited are such that their existence and operation have no explanation either full or partial in terms of other factors.'[34] The difference between these

[33] *The Existence of God*, pp. 74–5.   [34] Ibid. 75.

two is that a complete explanation may have a further explanation, though not by factors operative at the time; while an ultimate explanation has no further explanation at all.

Swinburne defines absolute explanation as a special case of ultimate explanation. Absolute explanation not only has no further explanation, but 'the existence and operation of each of the factors cited is either self-explanatory or logically necessary'.[35] However, he believes that no such explanations exist because nothing can explain itself nor, as we noted earlier, can anything logically contingent follow from something logically necessary. Both of these reasons for denying the possibility of absolute explanation find their force in the fact that he is speaking of causal explanation. Obviously something cannot cause itself; so it cannot be self-explanatory in that way. And, if explanation is defined in terms of deductive entailment, any entailment following from a logically necessary proposition must itself be logically necessary. But, since the universe is logically contingent, an explanation of the universe must also be logically contingent. Therefore, if something does exist with logical necessity, it cannot be the explanation of the universe (nor anything else logically contingent).

Swinburne is correct on this point: nothing contingent is entailed by anything logically necessary. It also follows that, in the context of a causal explanation where, as Swinburne argues, a full explanation deductively entails that which is to be explained, there can be no absolute explanation, if that which is to be explained is logically contingent. But it does not follow from this that God cannot be a logically necessary being. Even if we grant Swinburne's concept of explanation, this conclusion would not follow. He would need to show that, if God is a logically necessary being, God's choices and actions are logically necessary as well. This Swinburne has not done.

If we speak of God as a personal being, his choices, decisions, and actions must be contingent. This is entirely consistent with the claim that God is a logically necessary being. Though the logically contingent cannot be deduced from the logically necessary, the logically contingent can be deduced from the conjunction of a logically necessary truth, namely, God exists, and a logically contingent truth, namely, God had the

[35] Ibid. 76.

intention to create the universe. It is not from the sheer existence of God that the universe is deduced: rather it is the contingent action of the personal God which explains the existence of the universe. The crucial issue then is whether something can exist by logical necessity and at the same time be a person.

If God is a maximally great being, he necessarily exists. This will be problematic only if maximal greatness is incompatible with being personal. But, since the concept of maximal greatness is defined in terms of the personal qualities, such as omniscience and omnipotence, there is at least no obvious incompatibility present. The properties which are essential to being a person, such as having beliefs, appear compatible with the property of 'existing in all possible worlds'.

A similar controversy appears in Thomistic discussions of the concept of God. Change entails having the potential to change. Since God is pure act with no taint of potential, it is impossible that he should undergo real change. If God cannot change, how, the objection goes, can he act since agency seems to entail change in the agent? In order to cope with this question, various solutions are proffered which safeguard God's purity while admitting some kind of true relationship to the universe.[36]

A similar issue arises in Swinburne's account over the relationship between God's necessity and his personhood. It appears that he believes one cannot hold these two attributes together. And given his concern for explanation, he abandons logical necessity.

One does not need, however, to pose such stark alternatives. Once one separates the logical necessity of God's existence from the contingency of his actions, there is no need to deny that God is logically necessary. Only if one holds something similar to the Thomistic concept of God as pure act is one driven to the extreme conclusion that logical necessity and personality are incompatible. Once the two properties are properly separated, there is no need to believe that they are incompatible; God has both. Keith Ward puts it as follows:

As for the necessary not entailing the contingent, that is, of course, quite correct. It is, indeed, a particular form of the crucial difficulty about the relation of creation to necessity with which I am centrally

[36] Cf. Schubert Ogden, 'The Reality of God', in *The Reality of God and Other Essays* (London, 1967), 16–20.

concerned. It clearly requires making God, the self-explanatory being, contingent in some respects. . . . I think Swinburne's mistake, and that of most other theists who have discussed the issue, is to insist that God is either necessary in all respects, or contingent in all respects—just the ultimate contingent fact. Whereas . . . we can have both necessity and contingency in God. And we need both.[37]

The case against the logical necessity of God's existence, therefore, is insufficient to show that the concept is incompatible with causal explanation.

It is evident, however, that the logical necessity of God's existence cannot enter into the *explanans* of causal explanation. For that reason, it may be objected that, even if the concept of a logically necessary being is coherent, it is simply redundant. There is no need to postulate such a God because logical necessity can play no role in the explanatory power of a hypothesis. Hence, we return to a question posed at the end of the last section. There I maintained that Swinburne's argument against taking God to be a logically necessary being was inconclusive and that it may be possible to demonstrate the coherence of the concept of a maximally great being by giving an argument for the existence of one. But in this section I have agreed with Swinburne that, if the concept is coherent, the fact that God is a logically necessary being cannot be significant for causal explanation. In the next and final section I shall show that the conflict can be resolved.

IV

Traditionally God's logical necessity has played a central role in arguments for God's existence. Kant is correct when he identifies this concept of God as one core element in the teleological and cosmological arguments. As we saw earlier in this chapter, Leibniz completes the cosmological argument with a metaphysically necessary being, and Thomas with a being of pure Act.[38] The more contemporary arguments such as Swinburne's move away from the centrality of God's logical necessity toward the explanatory power of theism as a hypothesis where the necessity of God, even in its weaker form, has no role to play.

[37] *Rational Theology*, p. 8.   [38] See sect. i.

It seems to me that both positions are in error: the former because it makes God's logical necessity do too much and the latter because it makes it do too little. In contrast to the traditional arguments, one must admit that the principle of sufficient reason and the principle of existential causality are at best highly controversial and therefore inadequate as general proofs for the existence of God.[39] Against contemporary usage it must be admitted that necessity, namely, logical necessity, has a significant part in the explanatory power of theism.

To see this we might look again at the role of the logically necessary being in traditional arguments. At least two functions come to mind. The first is to halt the regress of causes. Of a necessary being no further questions can be asked. The second function is to provide a sense of ultimacy to the explanation. It eliminates any vagueness or ambiguity in the answer to the question 'Why is there something rather than nothing at all?' If God is personal, then we can speak of Him as the cause of the universe. And if God is also logically necessary, then we can speak of Him as the absolute explanation of the universe. This is a further explanatory function of the theistic hypothesis. There is no mystery about the ultimate foundation of existence, for causal questions and ultimacy questions come together in the one logically necessary person: God.

If God is, as Swinburne argues, the logically contingent ultimate brute fact of existence, there are some questions which even an appeal to God's existence cannot answer. Swinburne notes that science cannot explain why 'there are any states of affairs at all; it can explain only why, given that there are such states, this state is followed by that state'.[40] And he implies with this assertion that the existence of God can. The existence of 'any states of affairs at all' is too big for science and is therefore a starting point for the argument for theism. The way he states this, however, conceals a crucial ambiguity. If God is logically contingent, his existence is but one instance of the states of affairs which make up this world. Moreover, if his existence is a brute fact, his existence is a state of affairs which cannot be explained. Hence, in this sense, even the appeal to God cannot answer why there are any states of affairs at all. Swinburne

---

[39] See William Rowe, *The Cosmological Argument* (Princeton, NJ, 1975), 73 ff.
[40] *The Existence of God*, pp. 71–2.

admits that 'a priori the existence of anything at all logically contingent, even God, may seem vastly improbable, or at least, not very probable. (Hence, "the mystery of existence".)'[41] God's existence, therefore, explains not why there are any states of affairs at all but only why, given that there is an initial state of affairs, there is this particular set of state of affairs.

It is important to put this into the context of an integrative theistic explanation. The capacity of a world hypothesis such as theism to explain both causally and purposively is an aspect of the integrative power of the hypothesis. The logical necessity of God's existence represents a third integrative concept. Theism makes sense of the universe in part by eliminating the ultimate mystery of the universe. Many, sensing that there must be some ultimate purpose and ultimate ground for existence, ask, 'Why is there anything at all?'[42] Theism has always served to provide an answer to this sort of question, a question that Swinburne's strictly causal formulation of the theistic hypothesis cannot answer.

What is at issue here is the nature of the cumulative case for theism as an explanatory hypothesis. Normally, God's logically necessary existence is not seen as part of the argument for theism. The mistake is either to make the entire case for theism rest upon this claim, as in the ontological argument, or to allow it no part in the theistic hypothesis, as in Swinburne's inductive approach. If we can understand God's logical necessity as a significant component of an integrative explanation, we have the possibility of a more powerful cumulative-case argument than is heretofore available.

I have argued that God's logical necessary existence is neither incoherent nor explanatorily irrelevant. Its value is within a properly understood cumulative case for God's existence. In this context we can see how the ontological argument is supported by the other evidential considerations and it contributes to the explanatory power of theism. It is a mistake to consider the different arguments in isolation and to fail to recognize how they answer different questions and how they mutually support one another. Mackie, as noted above, makes

[41] Ibid. 130.
[42] e.g. Trethowan and Findlay. Cf. Ronald Hepburn, 'From World to God', in Basil Mitchell (ed.), *The Philosophy of Religion* (Oxford, 1971).

a step toward understanding the reciprocal support these arguments give each other. Given Plantinga's restatement of the ontological argument he questions whether it is reasonable to accept the premiss that God is a possible being. In his answer he appeals to the 'simplest' conclusion as the most justified. He argues:

Surely the more extravagant is that which asserts that maximal greatness is realized in some possible world. For this carries with it the requirement that a maximally excellent being—and, indeed, a maximally great one—should exist in every possible world, whereas the rival premise that no maximality is realized in some possible world, still allows maximal excellence to be realized in some possible worlds though not in others. The latter, then, is less restrictive, less extravagant, and so on very general grounds the more acceptable.[43]

Mackie is correct as far as he goes. The more 'extravagant' hypothesis is less simple and, for that reason, less acceptable. He bases his conclusion, however, on too narrow a base. Once the overriding concern becomes one of evidence, it is simply false to imply that simplicity would be the sole factor in deciding the reasonableness of accepting God's possibility. A justification for the possibility of God will incorporate all the evidence and exploit all the resources of explanatory power the theistic hypothesis may have. This will include not only the simplicity of the hypothesis, but also the capacity of theism to answer questions about the cause of the universe and the meaning of existence.

These considerations are important with respect to the nature of God as a logically necessary being. Given that theism is a causal explanation of the universe, it is essential that God has the ability to make contingent choices and is free to do or to refrain from acting. In these respects God's choices are contingent. But, if God is not also a logically necessary being, theism loses some of its integrative power, for it does not answer the most ultimate questions about the nature of existence.

Thus, we can accept that logically contingent propositions cannot be entailed by logically necessary ones and can, nevertheless, deny Swinburne's conclusion that God cannot be logically necessary. Though God's intentions, beliefs, and choices

[43] *The Miracle of Theism*, p. 61.

cannot be logically necessary and also enter into the *explanans* of a causal· explanation, a further aspect of the cumulative explanatory nature of theism is its ability to answer questions of ultimacy as well. And, because explanations of this type are not causal, the explanatory relation between *explanans* and *explanandum* is not represented by deductive entailment and, therefore, not subject to the objection Swinburne makes.

Certain kinds of question can be answered by postulating God's logically necessary existence, but not by taking his existence to be logically contingent. This feature of the theistic hypothesis constitutes only a part of the case for the existence of God. The argument for God's existence is a many-sided affair. Theism explains a range of phenomena in a variety of ways. The logical necessity of God's existence is not needed to explain everything, but only some aspects of existence which would not otherwise be understandable.

In this chapter I have defended the notion, *pace* Swinburne, that God is a logically necessary being and have argued that, so construed, this concept of God has explanatory power (though not in the context of a purely causal explanation). However, my conclusion here, especially combined with the conclusion from the last chapter, may seem too controversial: the concept of a logically necessary person as the central integrating concept of theism may clash too strongly with what is understood as the traditional concept of God. In the final chapter, therefore, I shall examine the relationship between the concept of God and the argument given here in support of God's existence.

8

THE CONCEPT OF GOD AND
NATURAL THEOLOGY

IN the previous two chapters I have explored the fundamental integrative concept of theism: God conceived of as a person existing by logical necessity with specific purposes for the creation of the universe. This particular concept of God, I believe, provides maximal integrative power, and, for that reason, it may be argued that it gives the best integrative explanation. However, the reader may find this description of God problematic and may question my identification of it with traditional theistic belief about God. Many may contest, for example, the relatively straightforward description of God as a person as being too anthropomorphic. Patrick Sherry makes this observation very pointedly in his criticism of Swinburne. He writes: 'The spirit described in Swinburne's thought-experiment sounds more like a super-Frankenstein than the God of Abraham, Isaac and Jacob.'[1]

The problem with this criticism, however, is that it ignores the relationship between the argument one uses to support belief in God and the concept of God that is used. I made a similar point earlier against Wiles and Flew. I argued that both fail to make crucial distinctions between concepts of God that must accompany different kinds of natural theology.

The importance of this observation lies in the light that it sheds on the concept of God. An integrative explanatory argument for the existence of God is based upon several different kinds of explanatory power which come together in one integrative hypothesis. Thus, theism explains the causal origin of the universe; it explains the significance of the universe; it answers fundamental questions such as 'Why something rather than nothing?' In order to carry out all these explanatory func-

[1] *Spirit, Saints and Immortality* (London, 1984), 13.

tions, the objects postulated in the hypothesis must be related in some way to causality, purpose, and ultimacy. If they are not, the hypothesis cannot fulfil its designed explanatory role. It is in this light that I propose to speak of God as a person: the concept of person (more specifically, the concept of a logically necessary person) seems to combine most adequately the features needed for this explanatory task.

The tie between the concept of God and the argument supporting the existence of God implies two things about the criticism of a concept of God. The first concerns the coherence of the concept. Often it is assumed that the coherence of a concept must first be demonstrated, and only then is it possible to question whether the concept is or is not instantiated in reality. However, such a project will be difficult because the concept of God is developed as the argument itself is developed, and radically different concepts of God may result from different kinds of argument.

The second implication concerns the development of the concept itself. Given the relation between concept and argument, the argument deployed sets constraints on what can be said about God. Thus, I assert, for example, that God is a person because God's causal activity explains the existence of the universe and God's will explains the meaning of life. However, if I had severed the conceptual tie and had postulated a God that could not act or had no purposes, then that argument could not establish the existence of that God. There must be some connection between the kind of argument given and the content of the concept itself, and this connection places limits on what can be said about God given a particular argument.

In this chapter I shall indicate the importance of the conceptual tie between concept and argument by examining a number of objections that can be raised against the concept of God as a person.

I

Sutherland and Mackie provide specific criticisms against using the concept of a person to describe God. Sutherland attacks the coherence of the concept of God as a person, and

Mackie rejects the existence of God due to the oddness of the kind of person God would have to be.[2] Both illustrate the failure to take into account the nature of the suggested argument for the existence of God. I have argued that the concept of God serves as an integrative concept used to explain various phenomena. Thus, on this view, God is introduced as a hypothetical entity. Neither Sutherland nor Mackie, however, takes this into account seriously. Both question the applicability of the concept of person to God because of the disanalogy between human persons and God. This overlooks the hypothetical character of the concept of God.

Sutherland criticizes traditional attempts to address the problem of evil because they approach evil with a presupposed theology. Evil, given the traditional view of God, must be accounted for, and this takes the argument in one or both of two directions. Either we produce 'morally sufficient reasons' for God's action or we appeal to mystery. Sutherland identifies Roy Holland, Hick, Mitchell, and Swinburne, along with anyone who engages in the traditional attempt to vindicate the goodness of God, as philosophers who fall into this trap.[3] He uses the views of John Hick to illustrate the problem. Hick argues that the inexplicability of evil is a virtue of Christian theism. It fits, he says, with the '"Irenaean strand of Christian thought" in so far as it is one element of what makes this world a vale of soul-making'.[4] According to Sutherland, Hick is driven to this conclusion because he begins with an 'established theology'. 'Such a definition [of God]', Sutherland notes, 'drives us, in the face of evil, to the dual expedients of looking for "morally sufficient reasons" and also underwriting the need for giving a central place *in this context* to mystery.'[5]

Sutherland tries to highlight the connection between what we think we know about God and the need to construct a theodicy.[6] The need to have a theodicy follows directly from the assumption that God is an individual who acts in history. On

[2] The issue of the coherence of the concept of God has proved especially fruitful in recent philosophy of religion. Issues around which significant literature has grown to enormous proportion are foreknowledge and free will, disembodied existence, the problem of evil, and necessary existence.

[3] Sutherland, *God, Jesus and Belief: The Legacy of Theism*, pp. 22 and 25.

[4] Ibid. 26.

[5] Ibid. 27.   [6] Ibid.

this model God is a morally responsible person. This in turn creates the tension between the facts of existence and the belief that God exists. Sutherland rejects this presumption and begins the theological task with the facts of evil rather than with a belief about God.[7] Ultimately he concludes that no theodicy actually delivers what is needed, and, for that reason, he seeks an alternative concept. In the course of arguing this, he develops a number of criticisms of the concept of God as person.

First, Sutherland believes that there is something arbitrary about the way theists approach the problem of evil. Why distinguish, for example, the problems raised by the existence of evil from those brought about by the supposed nature of God? As Sutherland sees it, if the theist were forced, at the point of explaining the nature of God, to admit the sort of mystery needed to deal with the problem of evil, he would have to give up that concept of God. Sutherland summarizes the problem this way:

If we are to invoke the ideas of mystery and incomprehensibility at all, by what criteria do we decide when to appeal to them? There is something unacceptable about the tendency to invoke them in response to the questions raised by evil and suffering while apparently finding less difficulty in the *intellectually* equally problematic questions of the nature of God.[8]

Secondly, Sutherland addresses two different conceptions of God's relation to the world. The first is the traditional assertion that God is timeless. The second is the more recent affirmation that God is in time but 'everlasting'.[9] If God is timeless, then, according to Sutherland, it is impossible to attach any sense to the idea that God is personal. It makes no sense, in his view, to say that, if he is timeless, God knows or acts. The problem, Sutherland claims, lies with the notion of timeless action. He argues: 'Actions essentially belong to time. They involve change, and as such are receptive of being located in a

---

[7] Ibid. 20.   [8] Ibid. 28.

[9] The idea is not new, but the widespread acceptance of it is. Cf. Nicholas Wolterstorff, 'God Everlasting', in Clifton J. Orlebeke and Lewis B. Smedes (eds.), *God and the Good: Essays in Honor of Henry Stob*, (Grand Rapids, Mich., 1975), reprinted in Stephan M. Cahn and David Shatz (eds.), *Contemporary Philosophy of Religion* (Oxford, 1982), 77–98.

time-series. . . . Here we arrive at the heart of the limitations which the concept of timelessness . . . imposes upon the idea of God. It excludes the possibility of action, not just *corporeal* action, but *any* action.'[10]

He argues similarly against the concept of God as ever-lasting. Even if God is in time, the coherence of the divine attributes is threatened. Humans, he claims, have certain ways to distinguish remembering the past from experience of the present. A different degree of certainty attaches to our knowledge of the past than to our knowledge of the present. He writes: 'aware of our own fallibility . . ., it just is the case, and reasonably so, that we are prepared to attach a greater degree of certainty to our knowledge claims about what we are attending to now, than to our knowledge claims about what we were attending to yesterday.'[11]

Furthermore, we distinguish remembering the past from experiencing the present on the basis of the checks we have for justifying a claim about the past. Knowledge claims about the present appeal to close attention to the experience of the present. With remembering, in contrast, a series of checks is available, and 'in the absence of these we should not be inclined to talk of knowledge.'[12] For example, we may appeal to reports of the experience of others. Sutherland concludes on the basis of these considerations that the concept of God as everlasting is problematic, for God is not in a position to 'distinguish between remembering an event and being aware of an event'.[13] God's knowledge is immediate and involves no checks of any kind. Sutherland asks a rhetorical question:

If, as is being postulated, God's knowledge is immediate in the sense of not even being mediated through sense organs, and if also it is direct in the sense of by acquaintance rather than by descrip-tion, is there anything in the manner or content of being aware which for such a knower, could differentiate between rehearsing or recalling the past and being aware of the continuing present?[14]

The answer is certainly negative. The necessary checks are not there, and, therefore, no sense, he believes, can be made

---

[10] *God, Jesus and Belief*, p. 56.   [11] Ibid. 60.   [12] Ibid. 61.
[13] Ibid. 61–2.
[14] Ibid. 62.

of the distinction between knowing the past and knowing the present for an omniscient, everlasting being.[15]

Sutherland's criticisms identify problems which stem from the acceptance of the traditional concept of God as an individual with certain properties, such as infinite goodness and knowledge. His project has not been to reject the concept of God altogether, but rather to reject the traditional concept. These problems, he believes, are peculiar to the attempt to work out the traditional concept of God.

Mackie, in contrast to Sutherland, takes for granted the coherence of the concept of God as a person. He argues that we can in fact conceive of God on the analogy of human persons. So, for example, with reference to the idea of nonembodied existence, he makes this claim:

We know, from our acquaintance with ourselves and other human beings, what a person is—a person, as Swinburne explains, in the ordinary modern sense. Although all the persons we are acquainted with have bodies, there is no great difficulty in conceiving what it would be for there to be a person without a body: for example, one can imagine oneself surviving without a body, and while at present one can act and produce results only by using one's limbs or one's speech organs, one can *imagine* having one's intentions fulfilled directly, without such physical means.[16]

---

[15] Ibid. 63. Sutherland has objections to the idea of God as an everlasting being 'acting' as well. The general problem Sutherland finds is that God's actions are incredibly hard, almost impossible, to individuate (p. 65). Criticizing Swinburne's analysis of God's activity he notes: 'whereas Swinburne seems to limit the activity of God to bringing about the effects of, for example turning the ignition-key, the very act of turning the ignition-key itself requires the operation of natural laws which connect the movements of nerve-endings, bone, muscle and so on' (p. 65). The problem will be that in every one of an individual's actions—here, the turning of the ignition-key—a concomitant action of God's must take place. This is true of this single action and is also the case in the sum of individual actions which occur all the time. The idea of God's activity gets swallowed up by the sheer number of 'acts of God' necessary to keep the universe going and by the vast area over which the action must occur. As Sutherland comments, 'There is no sense in which such an omnipotent temporal being can be described as having a unique relationship to the area of history—his and ours—concerned. There comes a point where the sheer volume of "God's activity" so detaches the idea of "an act" even from basic notions such as "awareness" and "attention", that the attempt to understand how the other more complex elements of the concept of action apply to "an act of God" becomes a task which has no shape' (p. 67). Cf. Wiles, *The Remaking of Christian Doctrine*, pp. 37–8.

[16] *The Miracle of Theism*, pp. 1–2.

So Mackie from the beginning does not find the concept of God as a person problematic. What he finds difficult to accept is the evidential support for the analogy.

The problem for Mackie is the strangeness of such a person as God is said to be. He objects, more specifically, to the idea of non-embodied causation. Though it is clear that we can imagine it, it is highly improbable that it exists, relative to what we know about the universe. All our knowledge of causal interaction between persons and the world involves embodied persons. The concept of God requires that there be non-embodied causal interaction. Mackie writes:

And the key power ... is that of fulfilling intentions *directly*, without any physical or causal mediation, without materials or instruments. There is nothing in our background knowledge that makes it comprehensible, let alone likely, that anything should have such a power. All our knowledge of intention-fulfilment is of *embodied* intentions being fulfilled *indirectly* by way of bodily changes and movements which are *causally* related to the intended result, and where the ability thus to fulfil intentions itself has a *causal history*, either of evolutionary development or of learning or of both.[17]

The alleged naturalness and intelligibility of the connection, according to Mackie, is illusory.[18] Our idea of direct intention-fulfilment, he believes, comes about by neglecting the dependence of the action on the physical means to achieve it. And these are very complex. He sums his argument up and states:

we have no right to abstract from what is really such a complex process the simple relationship which is all that ordinarily interests us, and to use this as a familiar model for an intelligible immediate efficacy of intentions, to be employed in constructing personal explanations elsewhere, in the supposed creative and governing activity of a god.[19]

Mackie concludes that the prior probability of theism is very low, and hence he rejects theism altogether: 'In the end, therefore, we can agree with what Laplace said about God: we have no need of that hypothesis.'[20]

These two writers, Sutherland and Mackie, represent two different ways of objecting to the concept of God as a person. One is conceptual, and the other is evidential. Each identifies

---

[17] *The Miracle of Theism*, p. 100.   [18] Ibid. 129.   [19] Ibid. 129–30.   [20] Ibid. 253.

THE CONCEPT OF GOD AND NATURAL THEOLOGY

significant issues, but neither takes into account one of the most important considerations involved in the discussion, namely, that the concept of God is introduced as part of an explanatory hypothesis. This, when taken into account, diminishes the force of both their objections.

As part of a hypothesis, either a world hypothesis or a more narrowly conceived hypothesis, the concept of God is introduced as a theoretical entity postulated to explain various phenomena.[21] The analogy with scientific theories at this point is very instructive. Scientific progress depends on introducing new kinds of theoretical entity, and, simply because the concepts involved describe new and extraordinary kinds of theoretical entity, these will commonly conflict with our ordinary concepts. However, such concepts are not rejected on the basis of their oddness. Models, metaphors, and analogies are essential to the scientific endeavour. In the nature of the case there are conceptual discrepancies between the thing signified and the model, metaphor, or analogy used, and, for that reason, the latter break down at some point or the other.[22] But that is just what models, metaphors, and analogies do. Atoms thought of something like billiard balls, for example, are postulated to account for the properties of atomic interactions. Atoms exhibit only some of the properties of billiard balls and not others. The disanalogies do not bear any significant weight in the justification of these hypotheses because the models are utilized to *extend* knowledge. Conceptual disanalogies are expected in the scientific context, and, I believe as well, they ought also to be expected in the context of an argument which introduces God as an explanatory hypothesis.

It is important to distinguish this use of analogy from the traditional Thomistic doctrine of analogy. I noted above that Thomas offers the doctrine as a solution to a problem arising out of the metaphysical analysis he uses to prove God's existence. If we reject the metaphysics, we have no reason for

[21] In this instance we are postulating explanations for *global* features, those things too big or too odd for science to explain. Cf. Swinburne, *The Existence of God*, pp. 71–2.

[22] The idea is that the referent of the analogy is not meant to be identical with the analogue. The use of models, analogies, and metaphors is crucial to both science and religion. Janet Martin Soskice has written a valuable essay which examines the role of metaphor in science and religion. See *Metaphor and Religious Language* (Oxford, 1985), 118–62.

accepting the same sort of doctrine of analogy. Hence, the present position does not posit a doctrine of analogy for the same reasons as Thomas.[23] By postulating the existence of God, we provide an explanation for the existence of, among other data, the complex physical world. We introduce God as the theoretical entity which seems most adequate for the purpose of explaining. We do not presuppose that the reality behind the theoretical term is beyond conceptualization and, therefore, we do not need a doctrine of analogy of the kind found in Thomism to understand how reference occurs. The concept of God as a person is intended to be a genuine description. We generate new concepts using analogies, along with models and metaphors, which help extend our knowledge. This use of analogy is not an attempt to explain how reference occurs, rather it is a deliberate stretching of the meanings of old concepts to create new ones which are adequate for the needs of the explanatory hypothesis.

If we take into account that the concept of God is introduced in the context of an explanatory theory, then we can see that these objections, both conceptual and evidential, are misguided. Sutherland is very imprecise in the way he addresses the concept of God. He objects to traditional approaches to theodicy because they presuppose a particular concept of God, though he fails to allow that there are reasons for accepting that traditional concept. He approaches the discussion as a philosopher of religion, but he does not allow any weight to the fact that others such as Mitchell, Hick, and Swinburne do so as well. It is not that they come to evil with a preformed theology, but that they adopt the existence of a personal God as part of an explanatory system. Sutherland rightly questions the appropriateness of appealing to mystery in response to the problem of evil. Nevertheless, the impropriety he senses disappears when we recognize that the concept of God he criticizes is not arbitrary, but is part of an explanatory theory. In fact, it seems appropriate to ask him how he would answer the causal questions which that theory

---

[23] See ch. 6. See also the discussion of St Thomas's doctrine of analogy in David Burrell, *Aquinas: God and Action* (Notre Dame, Ind., 1979), 55–67. Gutting discusses Burrell's analysis of the doctrine of analogy. Cf. Gutting, *Religious Belief and Religious Skepticism*, pp. 50–78.

addresses without postulating God as an agent, i.e. as personal.[24]

This same complaint can be made about the other difficulties which he raises. He questions how a timeless God can act in the world and how a temporal God can know the difference between the past and the present. With these criticisms also Sutherland fails to account for the explanatory nature of the concept of God. As we have seen, since God is not a human person, some degree of disanalogy is to be expected. The contrast between the notion of God as timeless and God as everlasting is a case in point. Traditionally God is said to be timeless.[25] Many contemporary philosophers of religion, though, reject that doctrine for the same reasons as Sutherland does, namely, its inability to accommodate God's personal attributes.[26] The concept of God as everlasting is preferred for the same reasons. It is able to accommodate God's personal attributes. Sutherland, however, pushes the person analogy too far. He argues, for example, that God would have no checks by which he could distinguish the past from the present, and, for that reason, declares that it makes no sense to say that God can distinguish them. But he fails to recognize that it is precisely the fact of temporal location which allows God to tell the difference between the past and the present. If God is in time, by definition he experiences the present. He does not experience the past: he remembers the past. We individuate events by virtue of the temporal location. There is nothing more basic than temporal location by which God, or humans for that matter, can individuate events.[27]

Sutherland's conclusion shows that he attempts to press the analogy too far. However, theoretical terms often stretch the

[24] Sutherland conceives theology as the 'articulation of the possible'. As far as I can tell he does not address causal explanatory questions at all. Cf. Sutherland, *God, Jesus and Belief*, pp. 73–86.

[25] The best analysis of the idea of God's timelessness is Nelson Pike, *God and Timelessness* (New York, 1970). But cf. Eleonore Stump and Norman Kretzmann, 'Eternity', *Journal of Philosophy*, 78 (1981), 429–58.

[26] See Alvin Plantinga, *Does God Have a Nature?* (Milwaukee, Wis., 1980), 44–61.

[27] Sutherland's criticisms of the timelessness doctrine seem to presuppose the sort of answer I offer here. The lack of temporal location is the problem he sees with timelessness. It would seem that if we took the force of his objections and added some temporal dimension to God then the conceptual problems concerning activity and knowledge would disappear.

meaning of ordinary concepts. In fact the concept of God in time provides the means of individuation necessary to speak of God's knowing and acting. Because God is not spatially located, significant differences exist between human persons and God. Nevertheless, there is enough continuity to ensure the intelligibility of the concept of God as a person.

Mackie, in contrast to Sutherland, accepts the intelligibility of the concept of God as a person, though he believes the oddness of the concept makes it unacceptable. Obviously the criterion of fit has its place. This is especially true in contexts of ordinary science. However, at the point where new entities must be introduced, the criterion of fit has less and less importance. Swinburne's argument against the criterion of fit surely has force. He asserts that fit is less important the more scope the theory has. Therefore, with theories of the most general sort, there is nothing with which the theory can fit, since every other theory would fit within the scope of the more general theory.

The strength of this argument lies in the fact that theism is an explanatory hypothesis postulated to explain, among other things, the existence of human persons. Mackie demands that the prior probability of the theistic hypothesis be evaluated by the closeness of the analogy to human persons. But if God is called upon to explain the existence of human persons, Mackie's demand is unreasonable. Fit with the known characteristics of human persons cannot be a criterion. The point of using the concept of person is that it provides the most adequate analogy for the sort of causal agency required. Obviously significant differences between God and human persons exist, but we must take concepts from those we already have and stretch them if we are to make any progress at all in theorizing. Hence, we cannot expect the theoretical term to have exactly the same connotation as the concept might have in the context from which it is drawn. In that case it would not be an analogy. If God were exactly like a human person, he would be part of that which he is postulated to explain, i.e. he would be a human person. Mackie's evaluation of theism misses the mark because it fails to account for the context in which God is introduced, namely, as a theoretical term in an explanatory hypothesis.[28]

[28] It might be better to speak of agency, as Gaskin does, rather than persons. God is an agent who acts, speaks, etc. As Gaskin argues, every person is an agent, but possibly

II

Both Sutherland and Mackie's objections fail because they do not appreciate the argument in which the concept of God as a person is introduced. However, a different kind of criticism exists. Alternative concepts of God exist which emphasize the transcendence of God. These conceptions clearly distinguish God from the created order. In turn, this emphasis on God's transcendence leads to the most obvious criticism of the notion that God is a person, namely, that it is unacceptably anthropomorphic.

In this section, and the next, I shall assess two such alternatives to the description of God as a person. My intention is to examine the relationship between the particular concepts of God and the arguments which are used to justify those concepts. On the surface, alternatives to the concept of God as a person appear to hold together both a high view of God's transcendence and an adequate natural theology. The difficulty for these alternatives, however, is to provide an adequate natural theology without using a concept of God that is not modelled on human persons. Either an adequate natural theology will include some kind of causal notion that requires a genuine description of God as a causal agent, or the use of a concept of God which unequivocally distinguishes God from the created order will lack an acceptable supporting natural theology.

One alternative to the concept of God as a person which cannot be faulted on the count of anthropomorphism is that of John Hick. In a discussion on the personal nature of God, he concludes:

Is God, then, personal? No, in the sense that God, the Ultimate, *an sich*, is real beyond all interactive relationship with finite persons. Yes, in the sense that in addition to being authentically experienced in non-personal ways, the Ultimate is also authentically experienced in personal terms by many human persons.[29]

it is the case that not every agent is a person. Thus, we may preserve the personal characteristics which go with the concept of person while trying to prevent the hostility accompanying the idea of a person. I do not think it makes much difference, but if it is helpful, my discussion can be couched without loss in terms of agency rather than personhood. See Gaskin, *The Quest for Eternity* (Harmondsworth, 1984), 23–4.

[29] 'Is God Personal?', in Frederick Sonntag and M. Darrel Bryant (ed.), *God: The Contemporary Discussion* (New York, 1982), 179.

Hick claims that God in himself is not personal, though he certainly may be experienced as personal by humanity. About the concept of God he says:

Let us begin with the recognition, which is made in all the main religious traditions, that the ultimate divine reality is infinite and as such transcends the grasp of the human mind. God, to use our christian term, is infinite. He is not a thing, a part of the universe, existing alongside other things; nor is he a being falling under a certain kind. And therefore he cannot be defined or encompassed by human thought. We cannot draw boundaries round his nature and say that he is this and no more. If we could fully define God, describing his inner being and his outer limits, this would not be God.[30]

And he has also argued recently at length that religious experience is reason enough to believe that God exists.[31] He makes first some general points about the experience of God. The first has to do with the word 'God'. In the passage quoted above, he affirms the ultimate transcendence of God, that God is beyond any human conception. The word 'God' points to this ultimate transcendent reality but from a number of different directions. Thus, he believes, 'one person thinks of God as a great supernatural person, another as the infinite transpersonal Ground of all Being, or as the creative spirit; to one God is the loving heavenly Father, to another the stern Judge'.[32] The word 'God' does not have a single meaning, but is used in a whole host of ways.

The second point is that the question of God's existence is wrapped up with the question of the purpose and end of all existence. If God does not exist, life has no meaning. If God does exist, 'human life exists with the good purpose of God and that purpose will finally reach its fulfilment in a fullness of life and joy which are to us at present unimaginable'.[33] Thirdly, philosophical arguments do not prove the existence of God. Rather, they show the 'explanatory power of the concept of God by formulating fundamental questions to which the existence of God would constitute an intellectually satisfying answer'.[34] The fourth point has to do with experience. We normally trust experience which seemingly is caused by the

---

[30] *God and the Universe of Faiths* (London, 1973), 139.
[31] John Hick and Michael Goulder, *Why Believe in God?* (London, 1983).
[32] Ibid. 31.　　　　　　　[33] Ibid. 32.　　　　　　　[34] Ibid. 33.

'impact of reality outside us'. The principle is, as he says, 'that it is reasonable for us to accept as veridical what seems to be an experience of some aspect of reality outside us, unless we have reason to doubt it'.[35] Further, and this is the fifth point, this is the case even if there is a theoretical possibility that the experience may be wrong. Hick here claims a prima facie justification for beliefs based on cognitive experience.

The sixth point generalizes this to religious experience. People seem to experience God and, on the same principle, take their experience to be caused by God.[36] The seventh point has to do with differences between religious experience: 'If a limitless divine reality confronts and surrounds us, we may reasonably expect that we finite creatures will both conceive of it and experience it in all manner of partial, inadequate and perhaps distorted ways. Religious experience will accordingly be various, taking many forms, and always including a human contribution which influences the specific form that it takes on a particular occasion.'[37] Though he continues to accept its evidential value, Hick believes that the diversity of religious experience may raise doubts about the veracity of the 'realm of religious experience as a whole'. He says:

the fact that we make discriminations, trying to distinguish between genuine and false moments of religious experience, is not itself a reason to doubt the veridical character of this dimension of human experience as a whole. . . . It may still be the case that through the manifold hindrances and distortions operating at our human end of the process there is nevertheless a real presence and pressure of the divine Spirit upon the human spirit, causing the modifications of our consciousness which we then correctly describe as the experience of the presence of God.[38]

These points describe what seems to be Hick's most recent position on the nature and knowledge of God.[39] Unquestionably he holds a very strong view of God's transcendence and believes that his belief in the existence of God is justified on the basis of religious experience. Though he makes reference to the explanatory value of theism, he justifies his belief in God solely on the basis of religious experience. That is, he claims

[35] Ibid. 34.   [36] Ibid. 35.   [37] Ibid. 36.   [38] Ibid. 36–7.
[39] See Hick and Goulder, *Why Believe in God?*, and John Hick, *God and the Universe of Faiths* and *God Has Many Names* (London, 1980).

that religious experience is veridical and that it 'authorizes' his belief in God.

But, though Hick takes religious experience seriously, he does not take it seriously enough, for, if he holds this position consistently, he faces insuperable difficulties in adhering to his strong view of transcendence.

He claims that it is an epistemic principle about our experience that experience is to be trusted unless we have some reason to doubt it.[40] The example he provides is a simple perceptual claim: 'My present experience of the presence of the desk on which my script is lying is an example of an apparently cognitive experience. . . . And thus experiencing its presence is my reason for believing that the desk exists.'[41] Now if this is the proper analogy, we must reconsider which of our claims about God religious experience warrants. Hick addresses the issue of whether the diversity of religious experience negates the epistemic value of religious experience. Rightly he concludes that it does not. But he infers from the fact of such diversity that all religious experience points to the same reality in every case. And that conclusion he cannot arrive at simply on the evidence of religious experience.

If we look at one of Hick's own examples, this point becomes clear. He describes Jesus's experience this way:

He seems to have been conscious all the time of the presence of God as the most real of all realities. God, the heavenly Father to whom he spoke in prayer, in whose name he healed and pronounced forgiveness, and about whom he taught, was as real to him as the people he was talking to, or as the hills and Lake of Galilee.[42]

From this description of Jesus's experience it is evident that he did not experience the ultimate, as Hick describes it, but the personal God whom he addressed as 'Abba'. Whatever is made of Jesus's life, the records indicate that he believed God to be active in history in a direct way: God performs special acts in history; he leads Jesus into specific and particular situations, and so on. If this description of Jesus's religious experience is correct, Hick misrepresents its epistemic import. Given Hick's

---

[40] Hick's epistemic principle parallels Swinburne's principle of credulity. Cf. Swinburne, *The Existence of God*, pp. 254–71.

[41] Hick and Goulder, *Why Believe in God?*, pp. 33–4.   [42] Ibid. 38.

understanding of the cognitive value of experience, Jesus's experience is not prima facie evidence for the ultimate, 'beyond all interactive relationship with finite persons', but rather for the existence of God, the heavenly Father, who guides specifically and responds specifically to prayers and petitions. Hick makes an unwarranted jump from describing the experience of God as Father to describing the experience of God as the ultimate.

He defends his position by contrasting true epistemic experience with its human interpretation. Thus, religious experience will 'be various, taking many forms, and always including a human contribution which influences the specific form that it takes on a particular occasion. In other words, there may well be an element of human projection mixed with the all-important element of divine presence and projection.'[43] (It is not clear whether Hick intends to argue that religious experience is different from other kinds of experience, or that religious experience is but an instance of experience generally. I shall take him to be arguing for the latter: with his emphasis on cognitive experience, he uses examples to illustrate his argument which come from ordinary perceptual claims, and, thus, he seems to be placing religious experience within the wider context of experience in general.)

If Hick sees religious experience as an instance of experience in general, his distinction between cognitive experience and human interpretation seems to offer little if anything to his argument. If all experience is in some sense 'theory laden' or interpretive, then he must distinguish the interpretive element of experience that is 'epistemically significant' from the interpretive element that is 'epistemically irrelevant'. Since some interpretive experience is trustworthy and some is not, there must be some way to tell the significant experience from the irrelevant experience.

However, this kind of distinction cannot be made without weakening the prima facie warrant which attaches to the experience. Jesus's experience was of God the Father. The belief that God was especially guiding him is what the experience was prima facie evidence for. This much seems evident simply from the definition of cognitive experience. If Hick wants to show

[43] Ibid. 36.

that Jesus misinterpreted his experience, he has to show that something other than God caused Jesus's experience, that Jesus's experience came about for some reason other than how he described it.

Here Hick compromises his argument from religious experience. On his view Jesus's experience of God warrants the claim that God especially guided and directed his life. But Hick also wants to claim that Jesus's interpretation of his experience is wrong in a very profound way, since, on Hick's view, God does not intervene in the way that Jesus's interpretation of his own experience presupposes. Hick, therefore, asserts that Jesus experienced ultimate reality, which he then went on to interpret as the guidance of God the Father.

If this analysis of Hick's position is correct, it is hard to see what prima facie value, if any, Jesus's experience had. On the face of it, the experience was not of the ultimate, but of God the Father. If Hick wants Jesus's experience to be evidence that ultimate reality exists, he has to show how in fact it was the ultimate which caused the experience. But he cannot take as evidence Jesus's experience, for that seemed to be of God as Father. Hick needs some other knowledge of God than theistic religious experience to·support his belief that God is indescribable ultimate reality. In fact, he would need to exclude all religious experience whose description was of a particular object, be it God the Father as Jesus experienced him, the risen Christ as the Christian believer experiences him, or of Zeus as an ancient Greek may have experienced him. These experiences confirm the existence of the ultimate and not their more specific interpretations only if Hick can show independently of the experiences themselves that the experiences were caused by the ultimate reality. But to show this he cannot take these latter experiences at face value since, read in that way, they are actually inaccurate.

If religious experience supports belief in the ultimate, as Hick describes God, it is also evidence for God the Father, the risen Christ, Zeus, and so on. If Hick claims that one particular kind of religious experience, mystical experience, is veridical and the rest not, he must supplement his argument with some further evidence for his claim.

However, his stated views make any such explanatory argument difficult. He has some commitment to a divine reality which has created the world for certain purposes, and, indeed, he speaks at times of the value of theism for making the universe intelligible in respect of God's creation and purpose.[44] But this position does not square with his belief that God is indescribable. There is a real tension here. As we saw above, Hick denies that God is a person: we cannot describe God *an sich*. But in so far as he speaks of 'creation' and 'purpose', he just is speaking of a person. In a comment concerning religious language, he states:

Religious doctrines are not literal descriptions of the divine reality. Rather, they are symbols pointing to that reality by helping us to become conscious of it. And as symbols they have an optional character. For different symbol systems, drawn from different cultural sources, have developed within the various religious traditions.... And yet at the same time whilst these are two different languages, they are both languages about the same thing, namely the ultimate divine Reality, and are both means by which people seek to articulate their relationship to the reality.[45]

It seems that for Hick then adjectives such as 'creator' and 'designer' are optional. They are part of the symbol system which is a human projection and not something strictly speaking descriptive of divine reality. Hick cannot believe this and at the same time have a commitment to a doctrine of purposive creation which is in some way supposed to help explain existence.

A further and more serious consequence of this is that he has no basis for the claim that God causes experience at all. Once Hick begins to speak of God as 'cause' or 'creator' or 'designer', he introduces a degree of conceptualization which is incompatible with the basic understanding of religious reality as the indescribable ultimate. And if the belief that God is the creator of everything constitutes part of the cultural conditioning brought to religious experience by human projection, little content is left to the concept of God.

On the surface, as we have seen, Hick seems to combine a strong view of God's transcendence with a strong natural theology. However, on closer examination, he does not deliver.

[44] *Why Believe in God?*, 33 and 99.   [45] Ibid. 108.

Inconsistencies appear at the point where we attempt to bring together his concept of God and his natural theology. His understanding of transcendence places God beyond all human conceptualization. Nevertheless, he believes that we can justify our belief in God on the basis of religious experience. Hick cannot hold these two theses together. In the first place, his argument from religious experience will not, as it stands, justify a specific concept of God. His view of transcendence, if it is possible to justify such a view at all, must be based on a very narrow range of religious experience, and he must argue that other, more specific kinds of religious experience are much less trustworthy. For that reason the competing claims of religious experience force him into postulating some explanatory hypothesis which explains away the cognitive value of the competing claims but which also assures that the experiences remain experiences of divinity. Therefore, his argument for the existence of God cannot be based solely on religious experience. In the second place, given his strong view of transcendence, he cannot state that God is creator of the universe and cause of religious experience without contradiction. The assertion that God is beyond conceptualization and the assertion that God causes our religious experience are inconsistent. In the third place, Hick's description of God as the 'creator' of the universe is obscure. If such descriptions must be a part of the cultural interpretation of religious experience, then it is not clear to what he is referring as the 'creator', and his claim that ultimate reality is an explanatory hypothesis about the universe is unintelligible.

III

A second alternative to the concept of God as a person is that which may be called, roughly, the Thomistic, or classical, tradition. The Dominican Brian Davies, for example, criticizes Swinburne severely because his concept of God appears to make God an object in the world; that is, he leaves no room for God's transcendence.[46] On Davies's view, God's existence explains all things and cannot be a thing in any respect. Thus, he supports the Thomistic idea that God is not a member of any

[46] Brian Davies, rev. of *The Coherence of Theism*, *New Blackfriars*, 60 (1979), 81-3.

genus. Initially his objection to Swinburne seems to have force because of the desire, quite legitimately, to safeguard God's transcendence and sovereignty. But Davies approaches the concept of God by way of the *via negativa*, and, consequently, has very different philosophical requirements from Swinburne. Therefore, it is useful to examine the Thomistic concept of God as an alternative to the concept of God as a person.

By Thomism I understand that philosophical tradition which defines the concept of God in terms of a particular metaphysical understanding of pure actuality and which bases the argument for God's existence on the relation of dependence of non-self-subsistent being on self-subsistent being as worked out systematically by St Thomas.[47] The most difficult problem in defining this tradition is that, due to its richness, there are many different kinds of Thomists. Therefore, there is an inherent risk of misdescribing it. To avoid this I shall take one Thomist, Eric Mascall, as a representative of the tradition. The conclusions to which I come will to that extent be rather narrow and specific, but I believe they can be generalized to apply to the tradition as a whole. I select Mascall rather than some other representative of Thomism, or rather than St Thomas himself, for two reasons. First, Mascall develops his doctrine of God clearly and rigorously. This makes him much easier to understand than other varieties of Thomism. Secondly, he is cognizant of the modern philosophical concern for epistemology. For this reason he is more likely than St Thomas to develop a critical Thomistic position that includes both a high view of God's transcendence and an argument for God's existence that addresses modern concerns.

The idea which is fundamental to Thomism is that of God's self-subsistence. God is such that his very essence is to exist. This property distinguishes him from everything else. According to Mascall, finite, or contingent, beings have a real

---

[47] Thomas is not the originator of this concept of God. It is of Greek origin and has been present in Christian theology since its inception. Thomas is the most articulate exponent and the one to whom tradition bows. See Thomas Aquinas, *Summa Theologica*, ii, questions 2–10. See also H. P. Owen, *Concepts of Deity* (London, 1970). He provides a clear discussion of this classical concept of God. One might consult as well G. L. Prestige, *God in Patristic Thought* (London, 1952), and Christopher Stead, *Divine Substance* (Oxford, 1977) for an idea of the influence of Greek thought on early Christian theology.

distinction between *what* that being is, its essence, and *that* it is, its existence. This means that the existence of any contingent being is unexplained: it exists, but nothing about its essence makes this understandable. With God this is not the case. As a being of pure actuality, there is no distinction between what he is and that he is. This is the foundation, in Mascall's view, for the correlation between Thomism and the Scriptural text, Exodus 3: 14: God reveals himself as 'I AM', and that self-revelation is taken to mean precisely that in God essence and existence are identical; so that it is of the very essence of God to exist.

Mascall argues that the character of self-subsistent existence uniquely identifies God and distinguishes him from any finite being. We do not and cannot apprehend what God is in his essence, but in apprehending that infinite being is, we come to know certain of his attributes by deriving them from the identity of his essence and existence.[48]

He discusses the definition of divine attributes given by R. P. Phillips: 'those absolutely simple perfections, unmixed with imperfection, which exist necessarily and formally, though in a higher mode, in God'.[49] In contingent beings 'perfections' are limited. Creatures are good, but they have only finite goodness. God, in contrast, is identical with goodness; he *is* goodness and hence unlimited or infinite goodness.[50] In God these 'simple' perfections exist necessarily. Creaturely attributes are contingent. They could be otherwise than they are. On this Mascall comments: 'They can be increased and diminished, they can even be acquired and lost, without the being which is their subject ceasing to be the same being.'[51] God's existence, however, is identical with his essence. Thus, every property he has, or could have, he is. Otherwise, what he is accidentally would be something other than what he is essentially, and God for that reason would not be absolute.

Furthermore these perfections exist 'in a higher mode' in God. Because God is infinite being, perfections cannot be 'realized' in him in the same way as in finite beings. Perfections,

---

[48] E. L. Mascall, *He Who Is* (London, 1943), 116.

[49] R. P. Phillips, *Modern Thomistic Philosophy*, ii (London, 1935), 307, quoted in Mascall, *He Who Is*, p. 116.

[50] Mascall, *He Who Is*, p. 116.   [51] Ibid.

such as, for example, goodness, must be realized in God in a manner appropriate to his infinity. We cannot express exactly what this mode is, 'for it must clearly exceed the capacities of our understanding. All we can really say is that God's goodness is related to his infinite Being in a similar way to the way in which our goodness is related to our finite being'.[52]

God transcends finite reality, and Mascall, along with others,[53] describes this transcendence by reference to the concepts of pure actuality and self-subsistence. Further, commitment to these concepts explains why the Thomist tradition rejects any conception of God which portrays God as changing. If a being changes, then, on the Thomistic analysis, he would *ipso facto* not be God.[54] For change means to become: for something to change it must become something other than it is, either essentially or accidentally. A being which changes must have the potential to change, and, such a being cannot by definition be self-subsistent. Thus, Mascall rejects any belief other than that God is metaphysically immutable. He asserts:

The very essence of our argument has been that the only hope of explaining the existence of finite beings at all is to postulate the existence of a Being who is *self*-existent. A first cause who was himself in even the very least degree involved in the mutability, contingency or insufficiency of the universe would provide no more in the way of explanation of the existence of the universe than it could provide itself; such a God would provide a foundation neither for himself nor for anything else. Unless we are prepared to accept the God of classical theism, we may as well be content to do without a God at all. If we admit any dependence of God upon the world, the very basis of the arguments by which we have been led to him is destroyed; a 'first cause' who is not self-sufficient explains nothing.[55]

[52] Ibid. 117. This gives rise to the doctrine of analogous language. Mascall provides here an illustration of the analogy of proportionality. Cf. E. L. Mascall, *Existence and Analogy*, ch. 5.

[53] Cf. Owen, *Concepts of Deity*, p. 36: 'God's transcendence means that he is incomprehensible. Even if his nature merely differed from all other natures to a superlative degree we could not conceive it fully; but since his nature (being infinite and self-existent) differs in kind from all other natures we cannot comprehend him.'

[54] At least anything other than 'Cambridge' change. See P. T. Geach, *God and the Soul* (London, 1969), 71–2.

[55] *He Who Is*, p. 96. Cf. 'Admit the tiniest element of time into God's timelessness, admit the tiniest element of finitude into God's infinity, admit the tiniest element of dependence into God's self-existence, and the very existence of the temporal, finite and dependent world becomes altogether inexplicable and unintelligible' (E. L. Mascall, *The Openness of Being* (London, 1971), 173).

If 'God' changes, then he is simply one more contingent being in the universe which needs explaining. Existence would not be of his essence; hence, his existence would be, similarly, completely unintelligible.[56]

Mascall relates the concepts of non-self-subsistent and self-subsistent being to, what he calls, the 'existentialist approach' to natural theology. He distinguishes this approach from the essentialist approach.[57] The essentialist approach, which he identifies with the ontological argument, seeks to show that God exists by virtue of an analysis of the essence of God. This approach fails, he believes, for two reasons. The first is that it is based on acquaintance with God's essence, a capacity which is beyond the capability of a finite mind.[58] The second is that it assumes that actual existence can be included in the concept of an essence.[59] Though, he admits, the concept of existence can be included in the concept of God, it cannot be used to demonstrate that God exists. Thomas, Mascall believes, argues not that God's essence causes him to exist, but that his existence is identical with his essence, and the identity of essence and existence in God cannot be used to show that he exists.[60]

The existentialist approach, which Mascall also identifies with Thomas, begins with actually existing beings, not with concepts. Actual, concrete existence of finite beings leads us to the existence of self-subsistent being. Mascall takes great care in explaining what he means by this. In the first place he defends a view of perception that he calls 'critical realism'.[61] Critical realism asserts that there are extra-mental beings—that things exist externally to the mind—and that the human

---

[56] I put 'God' in quotation marks since for Mascall a contingent being could not truly be God.

[57] *He Who Is*, ch. 4; *Existence and Analogy*, chs. 2–4; *The Openness of Being*, ch. 3.

[58] Thus, he is in line with Thomas who says that, though God is self-existent *in himself*, he is not self-evident *to us*. It is a fault of Descartes's ontological argument in particular that it depends on our comprehending God. See Mascall, *Existence and Analogy*, pp. 28–33.

[59] *Existence and Analogy*, pp. 22–4. Mascall distinguishes existence *ut signata* and existence *ut exercita*. The ontological argument proves only that God cannot be thought of except as actually existing (*ut signata*), but that is different from proving that he actually exists (*ut exercita*).

[60] Ibid. 42.

[61] *The Openness of Being*, ch. 6. Mascall refers to his position as critical realism in the table of contents, but not in the chapter itself.

mind perceives them directly.[62] It is this latter premiss which is important. Mascall alludes to the scholastic understanding of perception: 'According to this view, there is (at any rate normally, for we are not here concerned with mystical experience) no perception without sensation . . ., but the sensible particular is not the terminus of perception, not the *objectum quod* . . . but the *objectum quo*, through which and in which the intellect grasps, in a direct but mediated activity, the intelligible extra-mental reality, which is the *being*, the real thing.'[63] For Mascall, when we perceive an object, we apprehend it 'as something in itself, as an *in se*', as something that is truly there and is as we perceive it.

In perceiving something, two characteristics of the object of perception are present. The first is that it is real, i.e. that it has 'concrete existence', and the second is that it is contingent, i.e. 'it might not and need not have been'.[64] By contingency, Mascall does not mean contingency in the sense of 'has not always existed' or 'will not always exist', as we might say that the computer I am using will not always exist and is therefore contingent. Rather, he makes the metaphysical point that a contingent being is 'non-self-explanatory' or 'non-self-existent'.[65] Though there is no logical necessity that a being exists, since it does exist 'it must either be the ground of its own existence or have the ground of its existence in something else'.[66]

It is this perception of contingency in the objects of perception which is the foundation of the existential approach to God as Mascall understands it. For Mascall the argument for God's existence is strictly speaking only effectual inasmuch as someone has apprehended this metaphysical contingency through perception. He describes the relationship between the experience of contingency and an argument for God's existence as follows:

We can, of course, formalize the process in a conditional syllogism in the *modus ponendo ponens*, as follows:

(Major Premise)   If there is contingent being, there is necessary being;

---

[62] Ibid. 98–100.   [63] Ibid. 98–9.   [64] Ibid. 109–10.
[65] Ibid. 110.   [66] Ibid.

(Minor Premise)   But there is contingent being;
(Conclusion)   Therefore there is necessary being;

but this is really misleading. For it is only through perceiving contingent being that we can be brought to affirm the major premise; and the minor premise having thus been given, the conclusion is given too. Everything depends on our capacity to apprehend the objects of our perception as they really are, in their radical contingency.[67]

It is not entirely clear in Mascall what the exact relation between concluding that God exists and this perception is. Minimally he argues that accepting the conclusion of the syllogism requires the mental grasp of the contingency of the object and its necessary ground in a single mental act, a 'contuition of God-and-the-world-in-the-cosmological-relation'.[68] One may need some prior discussion, but, even then, the purpose is to 'enable the mind to grasp what the contingency of contingent being really is', rather than to demonstrate the existence of necessary being by a formal argument.[69]

Mascall clearly believes that the connection between the concept of God and natural theology turns on the notion of self-subsistent being. Explanation of the existence of finite beings is only possible if self-subsistent being exists, and the concept of self-subsistence determines what can and cannot be said about God.[70] Much of the force of his discussion, therefore, is a function of the particular interpretation he gives to the question 'What explains finite reality?' Explanation, he believes, means giving an account of what causes *actually* existing beings to exist. It is this emphasis on the actual which distinguishes his (and, by his account, Thomas's) argument from others.

Mascall's interpretation of Thomas is lucid. He presents a metaphysical position which, to his mind, both addresses contemporary epistemological questions and also is continuous with traditional metaphysics. But there is a crucial tension, I think, in his argument which vitiates much of its prima facie plausibility. On the one hand, he speaks as if it is an explanatory argument. Necessary, self-subsistent being is the only possible explanation for contingent, non-self-subsistent being.

---

[67] *The Openness of Being*, pp. 111–12.
[68] Ibid. 111.   [69] Ibid.   [70] See ch. 7, sect. 1.

On the other hand, he appeals to this special mental apprehension of God-and-the-world-in-the-cosmological-relation
which he calls 'contuition'. The problem is that the two
appeals, to explanation and to contuition, do not sit easily
together, and, depending on which is emphasized, different
problems appear.

If Mascall takes contuition as the principal concept in his
natural theology, his argument takes on a particular character
which would not by itself support his concept of God. Contuition shows that there is some independent being which
supports the existence of the non-self-subsistent being. Mascall
believes that such a being must be one which is self-subsistent
and does not change. However, he cannot believe this on the
basis of the contuition. The nature of self-subsistent being is not
something which is given. This is especially critical since
Mascall wants to avoid ontologism, the view that we apprehend
God's essence directly. Mascall believes that we cannot apprehend God as he is: we must contuit the sustaining relation
between God and the finite particular. However, if we apprehend simply the finite particular and its being sustained, the
nature of the sustaining being, even if we want to say that it is
self-subsistent, is not given in the contuition. The nature of
self-subsistence would have to come through some further
explanatory theory about or interpretation of the contuition. In
that case the contuition itself would not lead directly to the
particular view of transcendence Mascall holds.

This problem has a further dimension. Particular contui-
tions involve particular finite beings. It is a further question
whether every finite being has a self-subsistent being as its
cause. The contuition reveals that a particular being is being
sustained. It is a factual connection between the sustaining
being and the non-self-subsistent being. But though this particular finite being has no essential reason to exist, there
appears no obvious way to generalize from it to all particular
beings except through some explanatory or interpretive theory.
Once this is done, the argument, the natural theology, is no
longer based simply on the contuition.

The tension becomes acute when we observe what Mascall
says about the contuition. It is absolutely fundamental for
anyone accepting the major premiss of the cosmological

argument.[71] His argument resembles the argument from religious experience in the sense that it is the apprehension of this sustaining relation which leads one to affirm the existence of the sustainer, and without that particular apprehension the argument would not be compelling. Thus, everything depends on the apprehension and not the argument. Mascall appears therefore to take the affirmation of God's existence out of the realm of discussion and argument. Rather, affirming the existence of God depends solely on having this special sort of apprehension. As was noted earlier, however, the apprehension itself is insufficient to support his view of self-subsistent being and transcendence.

He could, however, emphasize the explanatory value of theism rather than contuition, and, indeed, he seems to do this in places.[72] In this context his beliefs about self-subsistent being take on more content. He accepts the Thomistic metaphysical system within which the existence of God follows deductively. But, if the explanatory power of theism is emphasized, the character of his argument becomes significantly different, and the problem will be in finding some acceptable way to interpret it. The argument postulates a necessary condition for the existence of contingent being. It is part of the Thomistic metaphysical scheme that contingent beings need this sort of foundation. Otherwise, of necessity, they could not exist.

This notion of explanation has at least two problems. First, there is not a clear sense in which the sustaining relation between God and finite being can be evaluated as an explanation for finite being. Mascall asserts that God's existence is a necessary requirement for the existence of finite beings, but the strength of his argument does not lie in its explanatory power or adequacy, i.e. those things such as simplicity which we might ordinarily see as marks of a good explanation. Rather, it lies in

[71] H. P. Owen makes a claim similar to Mascall's. In the preface to *The Moral Argument for Christian Theism* (London, 1965) he states: 'However, the word "argument" can be misleading. I do not intend to offer a proof that will coerce assent by means of formal logic; for I do not think that such a proof is possible from moral or from any other premisses. Discursive thought, operating on non-theistic evidence, can give "reasons for" belief in God; but *belief itself cannot be acquired without an act of intuition*' (p. 7, my italics). What the relation is between the 'act of intuition' and reasons remains unclear. However, it seems paradoxical that he provides an argument which he does not believe will convince anyone.

[72] *The Openness of Being*, p. 173. Cf. *He Who Is*, p. 96.

the necessity of the connection it postulates. Furthermore, the importance of the necessary connection leads to the second problem. The sort of necessary connection which Thomism presupposes needs to be justified against Hume's criticisms. Conceptually, it seems possible that things exist uncaused or exist metaphysically contingently without any sustainer. On the surface, there is no compelling rationale, or, to be more specific, Mascall has given no rationale, for accepting the strong version of necessity which the Thomistic arguments assume.[73]

The conclusion which emerges from these observations is that the explanatory force of an argument like Mascall's does not lie directly in its postulation of the existence of God. That is, it is not God's existence which provides the explanatory power of Thomism. Rather, the explanatory power lies in the metaphysical scheme of Thomism itself. God's existence is a necessary part of the larger explanatory metaphysical scheme. In this sense, though Mascall's concept of God is a variation of the theistic world hypothesis, it is the metaphysical categories of act/potency and essence/existence which provide the integrative capacity of Thomism. If we are to assess the adequacy of the Thomistic tradition, it will be by assessing the adequacy of these metaphysical categories to integrate the data of the universe. It is beyond the scope of this chapter to provide an analysis and criticism of this particular metaphysical scheme, but it is important to note that this conception of theism renders contuition superfluous.[74] The strength of the argument for God's existence will be a function of the adequacy of the metaphysic. If Thomistic metaphysics are true, or reasonably justified, God's existence follows from the fact that there are changing things. No resort to a special mental apprehension is

[73] If such a rationale is possible, I believe that it will follow along the lines that I have set out in ch. 7.

[74] Interestingly Mascall defends the use of act/potency concepts as a *metaphysical* analysis of change: 'For unless we are prepared to say that, if X changes into Y, Y was potentially in X before the change, we shall not be recognizing that X has changed at all. We shall, instead, be assuming that X has been annihilated and that Y has been created to take its place, and we shall be substituting for the rich complexity of a universe which, with all its processes of generation and corruption, of life and death, persists through time a succession of discrete states without any real continuity' (*He Who Is*, p. 43). But it remains questionable whether this kind of metaphysical analysis is desirable.

necessary. Mascall's view of transcendence follows from the metaphysical categories alone. Self-subsistent being, whose essence is identical with its existence, is defined by the categories inherent in Thomism, and acceptance of such a view of transcendence depends on one's judgement concerning the reasonableness of the metaphysic.

It would seem, then, that Mascall, and the Thomist tradition to which he belongs, provides at best a highly controversial alternative to the concept of God as a person. On the one hand, if contuition is the basis for our assertion that God exists, there is no justification for Mascall's particular view of transcendence. The nature of self-subsistent being is not given in the contuition itself, but must be an interpretation of the contuition. On the other hand, his particular concept of God as self-subsistent being functions as an explanatory concept only within a highly controversial metaphysical theory. If Thomism is the best explanatory theory, Mascall's view of transcendence follows directly. But it is precisely this position that is controversial, for explanation of contingency is a concept with diverse meanings, and a metaphysical explanation of it need not be analysed in Thomistic, or Aristotelian, categories.[75]

IV

In these final paragraphs I want to comment on the importance of the preceding discussion for the development of the concept of God. In the first place the connection between the argument which one uses and the resulting concept of God as a person shows that the concept of God is not arbitrary. The use of an explanatory argument constrains what can be said about the *explanans*. In that light, the concept of God as a person is a natural extension of our ordinary concept of personal agency, though obviously the concept of personal agency is stretched in order to accommodate the kind of explanation theism is.

In the second place the concept of God as a person is more fruitful than may be recognized initially. One's initial response, as illustrated by the Thomistic reaction, may be to

---

[75] One important difference between philosophers on the nature of metaphysics is whether metaphysical systems should be seen as explanatory hypotheses or as derivations from first principles.

reject the concept of God as a person as being far too discontinuous with the traditional concept of God. However, this reaction ignores the lack of argued support for the classical concept of God itself. I have claimed, at least with respect to Mascall as a representative of the classical tradition, that the traditional concept of God is based on an unacceptable argument. Dissatisfaction with the traditional proofs is one reason why philosophers turn to explanatory arguments. If the move to explanatory arguments is made, however, then there must be a concomitant change in the concept of God that the argument supports. Any such change will bring the classical concept closer to the concept of God as a person.

This brings to the fore a third comment. In so far as alternative concepts of God are based on unacceptable natural theologies, it is not clear what alternatives to the concept of God as a person there are. The classical conception would seem to have prima facie weight simply for being the traditional view. But accepting such a concept of God would mean accepting either an extremely controversial metaphysical system or an extremely dubious contuition of God and creature. Neither of these routes is appealing. On the other hand, the sort of extreme transcendence characteristic of Hick's concept of God seems to outlaw altogether any argument for God's existence. If we accept the very intimate connection between the concept of God and the argument used in support of belief in God, then it is not clear to me what alternatives there are to the position taken here.

Finally, it needs to be said that, though in the context of an explanatory argument the meaning of ordinary concepts must sometimes be stretched, there is an intractable tension between the concept of God and the concept of person. I have argued that Sutherland and Mackie make too much of the disanalogies between God and human persons. The moral of their criticisms, however, is that the concepts cannot be stretched indefinitely. At some point meaning may be so stretched that it loses all common elements with the ordinary concept which provided the original analogy. For example, if you take away all temporal connotations from the concept of divine agency, I believe, you remove any recognizable resemblance between personal agency and divine agency. The objection to the coherence of such a position, it seems to me, would be legitimate. The problem remains, then, of how much stretching is legitimate and when do concepts get stretched so much that they become meaningless. My claim here is that this tension can be resolved only in the context of a judgement about the overall explanatory power of the postulated explanation: the more explanatory power a hypothesis has, the more acceptable will be the disanalogies between the *explanans* and the original concept with which the analogy is made.[76]

With this final comment we come full circle, for the question of the acceptability of a particular explanation brings us back to the issues discussed in the first part of this essay. In it I examined the evaluation of explanations and in particular the evaluation of explanatory systems such as theism. If, as I have argued, an informal approach is best suited for the task, there will be no clear-cut procedure for determining which concept of God is coherent and which is not. The final determination of the coherence of the concept will be inextricably intertwined with the informal judgement concerning the overall acceptability of the explanation. Hence, the question of the coherence of a particular concept of God and the question of God's existence constitute a unity which discussions in philosophical theology seldom recognize.

[76] Swinburne, *The Existence of God*, pp. 52 ff.

REFERENCES

ABRAHAM, William J., *An Introduction to Philosophy of Religion* (Englewood Cliffs, NJ: Prentice-Hall, 1985).
ACHINSTEIN, Peter, *Law and Explanation* (Oxford: Oxford University Press, 1971).
—— *The Nature of Explanation* (New York: Oxford University Press, 1983).
ADAMS, Robert, 'Must God Create the Best?', *Philosophical Review*, 81 (1972), 317–32.
AHERN, M. B., *The Problem of Evil* (London: Routledge & Kegan Paul, 1971).
BAKER, G. P., and HACKER, P. M. S., *Wittgenstein: Meaning and Understanding*, i (Oxford: Blackwell, 1980).
BARBOUR, Ian, *Myths, Models and Paradigms* (London: SCM, 1974).
BARKER, Stephen, *Induction and Hypothesis* (Ithaca, NY: Cornell University Press, 1957).
BARNES, Jonathan, *The Ontological Argument* (London: Macmillan, 1972).
BARTLEY, III, W. W., *The Retreat to Commitment*, 2nd edn. (La Salle, Ill.: Open Court, 1984).
BECK, Lewis White (ed.), *Eighteenth Century Philosophy* (New York: Free Press, 1966).
BROWN, Patterson, 'St. Thomas' Doctrine of Necessary Being', *Philosophical Review*, 73 (1964), pp. 76–90.
BUNGE, Mario, *The Myth of Simplicity* (Englewood Cliffs, NJ: Prentice-Hall, 1963).
BURRELL, David, *Aquinas: God and Action* (Notre Dame, Ind.: University of Notre Dame Press, 1979).
CHISHOLM, Roderick, *The Foundations of Knowing* (Brighton: Harvester Press, 1982).
—— *Perceiving* (Ithaca, NY: Cornell University Press, 1957).
—— *The Problem of the Criterion* (Milwaukee, Wis.: Marquette University Press, 1973).
—— *Theory of Knowledge* (Englewood Cliffs, NJ: Prentice-Hall, 1966).
CLARKE, Samuel, 'A Demonstration of the Being and Attributes of God', in *The Works of Samuel Clarke*, ii (London, 1738).
COHEN, L. Jonathan, *The Implications of Induction* (London: Methuen, 1970).

COPLESTON, Frederick, *A History of Philosophy*, ii (New York: Image Books, 1962).

CRAIG, William Lane, *The Cosmological Argument from Plato to Leibniz* (London: Macmillan, 1980).

DAVIDSON, Donald, 'Radical Interpretation', *Dialectica*, 27 (1973), 314–28.

DAVIES, Brian, review of *The Coherence of Theism*, *New Blackfriars*, 60 (1979), 76–83.

DILLESTONE, F. W., *The Christian Understanding of the Atonement* (London: SCM, 1968).

DOORE, Gary, 'Further Reasons for Agreeing with Hume', *Religious Studies*, 16 (1980), 145–61.

DURRANT, Michael, review of *The Justification of Religious Belief*, *Religious Studies*, 10 (1974), 233–6.

FERREIRA, M. Jamie, *Doubt and Religious Commitment* (Oxford: Oxford University Press, 1980).

FINDLAY, J. N. D., 'Can God's Existence be Disproved?' *Mind*, 52 (1948), 108–18.

FLEW, Anthony, *God: A Critical Enquiry* (La Salle, Ill.: Open Court, 1984); first pub. as *God and Philosophy* (London: Hutchinson, 1966).

GASKIN, J. C. A., *Hume's Philosophy of Religion* (London: Macmillan, 1978).

—— *The Quest for Eternity* (Harmondsworth: Penguin, 1984).

GEACH, P. T., *God and the Soul* (London: Routledge & Kegan Paul, 1969).

—— and ANSCOMBE, G. E. M., *Three Philosophers* (Oxford: Blackwell, 1967).

GOODMAN, Nelson, *The Structure of Appearance* (Cambridge, Mass.: Harvard University Press, 1957).

GOULDER, Michael (ed.), *Incarnation and Myth* (London: SCM, 1979).

GREEN, Michael (ed.), *The Truth of God Incarnate* (London: Hodder and Stoughton, 1977).

GUTTING, Gary, *Religious Belief and Religious Skepticism* (Notre Dame, Ind.: University of Notre Dame Press, 1982).

—— (ed.), *Paradigms and Revolutions* (Notre Dame, Ind.: University of Notre Dame Press, 1980).

HACKETT, Stuart C., *Oriental Philosophy* (Madison, Wis.: University of Wisconsin Press, 1979).

HARRÉ, Rom, *The Anticipation of Nature* (London: Hutchinson, 1965).

HARVEY, A. E. (ed.), *God Incarnate: Story and Belief* (London: SPCK, 1981).

HELM, Paul (ed.), *Divine Commands and Morality* (Oxford: Oxford University Press, 1981).

HEMPEL, C. G., *Aspects of Scientific Explanation* (New York: Free Press, 1965).

—— *Philosophy of Natural Science* (Englewood Cliffs, NJ: Prentice-Hall, 1966).

HEPBURN, Ronald, 'From World to God', in Basil Mitchell (ed.), *The Philosophy of Religion* (Oxford: Oxford University Press, 1971), 168–78.

HESSE, Mary, 'Simplicity', in Paul Edwards (ed.), *The Encyclopedia of Philosophy*, vii (London: Collier Macmillan, 1967), 445–8.

—— *The Structure of Scientific Inference* (Cambridge: Cambridge University Press, 1974).

HICK, John, 'A Critique of the Second Argument', in John Hick and Arthur C. McGill, (eds.), *The Many-Faced Argument* (London: Macmillan, 1968), 341–56.

—— *Evil and the God of Love* (London: Macmillan, 1966).

—— *Faith and Knowledge*, 2nd edn. (Ithaca, N.Y.: Cornell University Press, 1966).

—— 'Gaunilo and Anselm', in John Hick and Arthur C. McGill (eds.), *The Many-Faced Argument* (London: Macmillan, 1968).

—— *God and the Universe of Faiths* (London: Macmillan, 1973).

—— *God Has Many Names* (London: Macmillan, 1980).

—— 'Is God Personal?', in Frederick Sonntag and M. Darrel Bryant (eds.), *God: The Contemporary Discussion* (New York: Rose of Sharon Press, 1982).

—— (ed.), *The Myth of God Incarnate* (London: SCM, 1977).

—— and GOULDER, Michael, *Why Believe in God?* (London: SCM, 1983).

HOWICH, Paul, *Probability and Evidence* (Cambridge: Cambridge University Press, 1982).

HUDSON, W. D., 'Language-Games and Presuppositions', *Philosophy*, 53 (1978), 94–9.

—— *The Philosophical Approach to Religion* (London: Macmillan, 1974).

HUGHES, G. E., and CRESSWELL, M. J., *An Introduction to Modal Logic* (London: Methuen, 1968).

JANTZEN, Grace M., *God's World, God's Body* (London: Darton, Longman and Todd, 1984).

JEFFERY, Arthur (ed.), *Islam: Mohammad and His Religion* (New York: Liberal Arts Press, 1958).

JEFFREYS, Harold, *Scientific Inference*, 3rd edn. (Cambridge: Cambridge University Press, 1973).

JEREMIAS, Joachim, *The Parables of Jesus*, trans. S. H. Hooke (New York: Charles Scribner's Sons, 1955).

KANT, Immanuel, *The Critique of Pure Reason*, trans. Norman Kemp Smith (New York: St. Martin's Press, 1965).

KEMBLE, Edwin, C., *Physical Science: Its Substance and Development* (Cambridge, Mass.: Massachusetts Institute of Technology Press, 1966).

KENNY, Anthony, *The Five Ways* (London: Routledge & Kegan Paul, 1969).

KUHN, Thomas, 'Objectivity, Value Judgment, and Theory Choice', in *The Essential Tension* (Chicago: University of Chicago Press, 1977).

—— *The Structure of Scientific Revolutions*, 2nd edn. (Chicago: University of Chicago Press, 1970).

LAKATOS, Imre, 'Falsification and the Methodology of Scientific Research Programmes,' in Imre Lakatos and Alan Musgrave (eds.), *Criticism and the Growth of Knowledge* (Cambridge: Cambridge University Press, 1970).

LEIBNIZ, G. F. W., *Discourse on Metaphysics*, trans. G. R. Montgomery (La Salle, Ill.: Open Court, 1927).

—— *New Essays Concerning Human Understanding*, appendix 10, in John Hick (ed.), *The Existence of God* (London: Methuen, 1964).

—— 'On the Ultimate Origination of Things', in *The Philosophical Writings of Leibniz*, trans. Mary Morris (London: Dent, 1934).

LEVIN, Michael E., *Metaphysics and the Mind–Body Problem* (Oxford: Oxford University Press, 1979).

LUCAS, J. R., *The Freedom of the Will* (Oxford: Oxford University Press, 1970).

—— 'The Lesbian Rule', *Philosophy*, 30 (1955), 195–213.

—— 'The Philosophy of the Reasonable Man', *Philosophical Quarterly*, 13 (1963), 97–106.

MACKIE, J. L., *Ethics: Inventing Right and Wrong* (Harmondsworth: Penguin, 1977).

—— 'Evil and Omnipotence', *Mind*, 64 (1955), 200–12.

—— *The Miracle of Theism* (Oxford: Oxford University Press, 1982).

—— *Problems from Locke* (Oxford: Oxford University Press, 1976).

MASCALL, E. L., *Existence and Analogy* (London: Darton, Longman and Todd, 1949).

—— *He Who Is* (London: Longmans, Green and Co., 1943).

—— *The Openness of Being* (London: Darton, Longman and Todd, 1971).

MASTERMAN, Margaret, 'The Nature of a Paradigm', in Imre Lakatos and Alan Musgrave (eds.) *Criticism and the Growth of Knowledge* (Cambridge: Cambridge University Press, 1970) 59–89.

MELLOR, D. H., 'God and Probability', *Religious Studies*, 5 (1969), 223–34.

MEYNELL, Hugo, *The Intelligible Universe: A Cosmological Argument* (London: Macmillan, 1982).

MITCHELL, Basil, 'How the Concept of Sin is Related to Moral Wrongdoing', *Religious Studies*, 20 (1984), 165–73.

—— *The Justification of Religious Belief* (London: Macmillan, 1973).

—— *Morality: Religious and Secular* (Oxford: Oxford University Press, 1980).

MONDIN, B., *The Principle of Analogy in Protestant and Catholic Theology* (The Hague: M. Nijhoff, 1963).

MOORE, G. E., 'Is Existence a Predicate?', *Proceedings of the Aristotelian Society*, Supplement 15 (1936), 175–88.

NEWMAN, John Henry, *An Essay in Aid of a Grammar of Assent* (London: Longmans, Green and Co., 1901).

NEWTON-SMITH, W. H., *The Rationality of Science* (London: Routledge & Kegan Paul, 1981).

OGDEN, Schubert, 'The Reality of God', in *The Reality of God and Other Essays* (London: SCM, 1967), 1–70.

O'HEAR, Anthony, *Experience, Explanation and Faith* (London: Routledge & Kegan Paul, 1984).

OWEN, H. P., *Christian Theism* (Edinburgh: T. & T. Clark, 1984).

—— *Concepts of Deity* (London: Macmillan, 1970).

—— *The Moral Argument for Christian Theism* (London: George Allen and Unwin, 1965).

PEPPER, Stephen C., *World Hypotheses* (Los Angeles, Calif.: University of California Press, 1942).

PHILLIPS, D. Z., *The Concept of Prayer* (London: Routledge & Kegan Paul, 1965).

PHILLIPS, R. P., *Modern Thomistic Philosophy*, ii (London: Oates, 1935).

PIKE, Nelson, *God and Timelessness* (New York: Schoken Books, 1970).

PLANTINGA, Alvin, *Does God Have a Nature?* (Milwaukee, Wis.: Marquette University Press, 1980).

—— *God, Freedom and Evil*, Grand Rapids, Mich.: Eerdmans, 1978).

—— *The Nature of Necessity* (Oxford: Oxford University Press, 1974).

—— 'The Probabilistic Argument from Evil', *Philosophical Studies*, 35 (1979), 1–53.

—— 'Reason and Belief in God', in Alvin Plantinga and Nicholas Wolterstorff (eds.), *Faith and Rationality* (Notre Dame, Ind.: University of Notre Dame Press, 1983), 16–93.

PLATO, *Euthyphro*, in *The Collected Dialogues of Plato*, ed. Edith Hamilton and Huntington Cairns (Princeton, NJ: Princeton University Press, 1961).

PRESTIGE, G. L., *God in Patristic Thought* (London: SPCK, 1952).

RAMSEY, Ian, 'On the Possibility and Purpose of a Metaphysical Theology', in Ian Ramsey (ed.), *Prospect for Metaphysics* (London: George Allen & Unwin, 1961), 153–77.

REID, Thomas, *The Works of Thomas Reid, D.D.*, ed. William Hamilton (Edinburgh: Maclachlan and Stewart, 1863).

RESCHER, Nicholas, *Leibniz: An Introduction to His Philosophy* (Oxford: Blackwell, 1979).

RICHMOND, James, *Theology and Metaphysics* (London: SCM, 1970).

RORTY, Richard, *Philosophy and the Mirror of Nature* (Oxford: Blackwell, 1980).

ROWE, William, *The Cosmological Argument* (Princeton, NJ: Princeton University Press, 1975).

—— *Philosophy of Religion* (Encino, Calif.: Dickenson, 1978).

RUSSELL, Bertrand, and COPLESTON, Frederick, 'The Debate', in John Hick (ed.), *The Existence of God* (London: Macmillan, 1964), 167–91.

SHAFFER, Jerome, *Philosophy of Mind* (Englewood Cliffs, NJ: Prentice-Hall, 1968).

SHEPHERD, J. J., *Experience, Inference and God* (London: Macmillan, 1975).

SHERRY, Patrick, *Religion, Truth, and Language Games* (London: Macmillan, 1977).

—— *Spirit, Saints and Immortality* (London: Macmillan, 1984).

SOBER, Elliott, *Simplicity* (Oxford: Oxford University Press, 1975).

SOSKICE, Janet Martin, *Metaphor and Religious Language* (Oxford: Oxford University Press, 1985).

SPINOZA, Benedictus de, *Ethics*, trans. Andrew Boyle (London: Dent, 1959).

STEAD, Christopher, *Divine Substance* (Oxford: Oxford University Press, 1977).

STRAWSON, P. F., *Individuals* (London: Methuen, 1959).

STUMP, Eleonore, and KRETZMANN, Norman, 'Eternity', *Journal of Philosophy*, 78 (1981), 429–58.

SURIN, Kenneth, 'Theistic Arguments and Rational Theism', *International Journal for Philosophy of Religion*, 16 (1984), 123–5.

SUTHERLAND, Stewart, *God, Jesus and Belief: The Legacy of Theism* (Oxford: Blackwell, 1984).

SWINBURNE, R. G., *The Coherence of Theism* (Oxford: Oxford University Press, 1977).

—— *The Existence of God* (Oxford: Oxford University Press, 1979).

—— *Faith and Reason* (Oxford: Oxford University Press, 1981).

—— *An Introduction to Confirmation Theory* (London: Methuen, 1973).

—— 'Mackie, Induction and God', *Religious Studies*, 19 (1983), 385–91.

—— review of Basil Mitchell, *Morality: Religious and Secular*, *Journal of Theological Studies*, 32 (1981), 567–70.

SYKES, Roderick, 'Soft Rationalism', *International Journal for Philosophy of Religion*, 8 (1977), 51–66.

SYKES, Stephen, *The Identity of Christianity* (London: SPCK, 1984).

THAGARD, Paul R., 'The Best Explanation: Criteria for Theory Choice', *Journal of Philosophy*, 75 (1978), 76–92.

THOMAS AQUINAS, *Summa Contra Gentiles*, bk. iv trans. Charles J. O'Neil (Notre Dame, Ind.: University of Notre Dame Press, 1975).

—— *Summa Theologica*, ii (London: Eyre and Spottiswoode, 1964).

TOTON, René (ed.), *Science in the Nineteenth Century*, trans. A. J. Pomerans (New York: Basic Books, 1965).

TRETHOWAN, Illtyd, 'The Significance of Process Theology', *Religious Studies*, 19 (1983), 311–22.

VAN FRAASSEN, Bas C., *The Scientific Image* (Oxford: Oxford University Press, 1980).

WARD, Keith, *Holding Fast to God* (London: SPCK, 1982).

—— *Rational Theology and the Creativity of God* (Oxford: Blackwell, 1982).

WARNOCK, Mary, *Existential Ethics* (London: Macmillan, 1967).

WILES, Maurice, *Faith and the Mystery of God* (London: SCM, 1982).

—— *The Remaking of Christian Doctrine* (London: SCM, 1974).

WITTGENSTEIN, Ludwig, *Lectures and Conversations on Aesthetics, Psychology and Religious Belief*, ed. Cyril Barrett (Los Angeles: University of California Press, n.d.).

—— *Philosophical Investigations*, ed. G. E. M. Anscombe and R. Rhees, trans. G. E. M. Anscombe, 2nd edn. (Oxford: Blackwell, 1958).

WOLTERSTORFF, Nicholas, 'God Everlasting', in Clifton J. Orlebeke and Lewis B. Smedes (eds.), *God and the Good: Essays in Honor of Henry Stob* (Grand Rapids, Mich.: Eerdmans, 1975), repr. in Stephen M. Cahn and David Shatz (eds.), *Contemporary Philosophy of Religion* (Oxford: Oxford University Press, 1982), 77–98.

INDEX